MUSIC
RIGHT
and
LEFT

by

Virgil Thomson

GREENWOOD PRESS, PUBLISHERS
NEW YORK

26695

CONTENTS

PRELUDE

Ten years ago, as this book goes to the printer, I made my bow to the New York musical scene in a role I had not previously undertaken, that of a reviewer of music in the daily press. Misgivings were in my mind about my appropriateness for the task. As a composer of definite orientation about schools and styles, I had some fear lest inevitable offense to vested musical interests bring on battles that my employers might find inimical to a newspaper's duty, which is informing the public.

Such battles did not fail to burst. But considerably to my surprise, the editors of the *New York Herald Tribune*, far more used than I to public controversy, seemed less to be worried than interested. They found it only natural that differences of opinion should exist between their critical columns and the organizers of musical events. Their own aim, indeed, was early revealed to me as identical with my own. We were not interested in either backing or attacking, on principle, the Philharmonic-Symphony Society or the Metropolitan Opera Association or the commercial associations engaged in concert management.

We were simply informing the public, to the best of our ability, about the products offered by these groups, as well as by all others.

In my first years on the paper I layed about me a good deal, and the paper took the brunt of the counterattacks. With punctilious consideration for my inexperience, my employers actually kept from my knowledge the troubles I had caused them. Ogden Reid, the editor, Geoffrey Parsons, the chief editorial writer, Mrs. Reid, the whole editorial and business staff stood behind me. So did my music staff, headed by the devoted and impeccably informed music editor, Francis Perkins. At no time, in fact, during my ten-year association with the *Herald Tribune* have the editors interfered once with the statement of my musical opinions or offered me a directive along that line. Counsel I have received, and mostly I have had to ask for that, about the ethics of controversy and the amenities of public statement. But from the beginning it is I, not those who fancied themselves my opponents, who have had the paper's support.

Also from the beginning I have held to my line. That line assumes that a musician's account of a musical event has legitimate interest for readers. Personal tastes I consider it fair to state, because by admitting one's prejudices and predilections one helps the reader to discount these. I do not consider them otherwise interesting nor ask for agreement regarding them. Description and analysis, however, I have tried to make convincing and, as far as possible, objective, even when sympathy is present. My own sympathies, frankly, are normally with the artist. I try to explain him, not to protect the public against him, though preserving a status quo or protecting anybody's career is not my intention either. Neither do I think myself entitled to make out report cards. I do not give an examination; I take one. I write a theme about an occasion. If my remarks are not found apt, that is no fault of the subject.

Over the years, I do find, however, that my coverage has altered. At the beginning it was more catholic. I reviewed the big names and the little names, the old music and the new. Nowadays I pay less attention to standard repertory and standard soloists, to what one might call the nationally advertised brands. They get covered, of course; but I tend to leave these more familiar assignments to my ever-patient colleagues of the staff. I like to examine the newer trends, the nonstandardized musical life of outlying cities, experiments in the universities, everything that might be preparing the second half of our century for being different from the first. That is why the present volume has so much to do with the problems of modernism and so little with Marian Anderson or Toscanini.

With all the battles of modernism now long since won excepting that of the atonal style, the twelve-tone-row composition of Schönberg and his school has been of late a constant subject of my awareness. It is my firm hope that the latter part of our century will see the amalgamation of all the modernist musical techniques into a twentieth-century classic style. Such an evolution, indeed, has been in progress ever since the First World War. Whether any of the atonal ways, the most resistant of all to absorption, can be saved for posterity or whether, as many atonalists believe, this style must either kill off all others or wholly die is a matter of passionate preoccupation to musicians. A large part of the youth in America, in France, in Italy, in England, in South America has already placed its faith in the twelve-tone syntax. The question of its future, nevertheless, still burns. That is why I cannot keep from coming back to the subject again and again and why I hold by sharing my interest in it with readers.

Another subject that has been constantly in my thoughts, and in those of many another reviewer, is the future of opera in America. I have searched out novelty with hope, and I have watched with anxiety repeated efforts of the Metropolitan establishment to lift itself out of a stagnancy. Just now a new general manager, Rudolf Bing, is taking over that establishment. His intentions are certainly of the best, but nobody knows what he will be able to do with an impoverished and seemingly moribund institution. His mere presence, however, has rendered obsolete all preachments about the ineffectiveness of previous policies. I have omitted, therefore, most of my general articles about the Metropolitan and left merely some reviews of specific performances. If the coverage seems skimpy here, it has not been so, believe me, in my column.

My ten years on the *New York Herald Tribune* have been lively for all concerned and for me a happy decade. I have had some good fights, heard lots of beautiful music, made a few enemies and hundreds of friends. Earlier volumes of my collected reviews give a broader view, show more of the whole musical scene. This one, which includes reviews and Sunday articles published between October, 1947, and June, 1950, falls short, I realize, of being a full panorama of music at the half-century. It is rather a peep into certain forces at work, in my opinion, toward the realization of our century's identity. Those forces are abundantly present in our concert halls and opera houses these days; listening to and for them is a delight. They are not the only delight of musical attendance, but they are the chief source of that "strangeness in the proportion" that is ever the foretaste of beauty. The rest appears more and more to me, after ten years' press service, as not quite news.

V. T.

October, 1950
New York City

I. ORCHESTRAS AND CONDUCTORS

Conservative Institution

The symphony orchestra, among all our musical institutions, is the most firmly established, the most widely respected and, musically speaking, the most efficient. It is not, however, either the oldest or the most beloved. The opera and the singing society, I should think, have better right to the latter titles. Nevertheless, the orchestra is what all music, its prestige, its exploitation, and its teaching, turns round. It is the central luminary of our contemporary musical system.

Someone, I cannot remember who, suggested several years ago that the strength of the institution comes from the fact that the con-

1

cert orchestra is a representation in art, a symbol, of democratic assembly. Certainly it is so conceivable. And certainly its rise is contemporaneous historically with the rise of parliamentary government. The fact that its most glorious period, as regards composition, the working years in Vienna of Haydn, Mozart, and Beethoven, was a time when, in that place, there was no parliamentary government at all, does not disprove the identification. It merely suggests that the parliamentary ideal, as represented then by England, was strong enough to influence democratic-minded men everywhere and that its picturing through music, an art difficult to censor, is more than probable in a country which would not have tolerated at the time any such representation through the less hermetic techniques of painting and literature.

In any case, these men in Austria, not the composers of liberal England or of revolutionary France, transformed the court symphony into the popular symphony. Never again, after they had lived, was the symphony an elegant or decorative form. It was larger, louder, more insistent, more humane, broader of scope, and definitely monumental. Its performance ceased to be a private entertainment and became a public rite. Also, there has remained with the symphony ever since an inalienable trend toward, in the broad sense, political content.

Professional symphony orchestras today remain associated with a political unit, the city. They are a privilege and symbol of civic pride. States and central governments rarely support them. Even municipalities do not like contributing taxpayers' money to them, though in a few American cities—Baltimore, Indianapolis, and San Francisco—there is a budgetary provision for such aid. Normally they are a civic proposition, and their deficits are met by public-spirited citizens. Rarely are great orchestras associated with our religious or scholastic foundations (as our finest choruses are more often than not) or directly with the world of big business and finance and fashion (as our best opera companies have always been). They are wedded to our great cities. They are monuments of civic pride and symbols not only of musical achievement but of their communities' whole cultural life.

2

There are really two kinds of orchestras, the monumental and the directly functional. The latter kind exists in large numbers connected with educational institutions and with the amateur musical life of neighborhoods and of semirural communities. In 1937 there were about 30,000 of these in the United States alone. Their chief purpose is the musical training or musical enjoyment of the players, though they also provide in increasing numbers nowadays professional players to what I call the monumental orchestras. The latter are strictly professional and perform only for the edification of the listener.

The functional orchestras, being educational in purpose, play a larger repertory than the others do. And their style of execution is less standardized. The monumental orchestras, being more ceremonial by nature, are highly standardized in both repertory and execution, internationally standardized, in fact. The players, the conductors, the pieces played (save for a very small number that represents local taste only) can be removed from one orchestra and inserted in another anywhere in the world. Even language is no barrier to rehearsal efficiency. Indeed, it is exactly their international standardization that enables our orchestras to represent localities, to symbolize to the whole world the cultural level—by internationally recognized standards—of the particular city that supports any one of them.

The civically supported symphony orchestra is the most conservative institution in the Western world. Churches, even banks, are more open to experiment. The universities are daring by comparison. This does not mean that new music does not get played by the orchestras. The rendering of contemporary works along with familiar classics is one of their firmest traditions. No orchestra can live that plays only the music of dead composers. As a matter of fact, no orchestra ever essays so radical a policy. The public objects to modern music, naturally, because modern music, however great intrinsic musical interest it may present, simply can never compete as edification with the hallowed past. But the same public that objects to hearing modern music objects far more vigorously to being deprived of the privilege. Just as the musical execution of our symphony orchestras is the most conservative and correct that money can buy, so also is the repertory they play, a certain appearance of musical progressiveness being required by tradition itself.

The encouragement of musical advance, however, is not the chief purpose of symphony orchestras. The first-line trenches of that lie elsewhere. They lie in many places, but always the rapidest progress of musical invention takes place where the attention of so large and so pious a public is not present to discourage the inventor. Small groups of musicians working under private or university patronage can produce more novelty in a year than will be heard at the subscription concerts in twenty. Invention takes place sometimes, even under the very eye of a large public, provided that public is looking at something else.

If theatrical entertainment is there to give novelty a *raison d'être,* as at the ballet or at the opera, or if the occasion is not too respectable socially, as in jazz dives, then the circumstances for musical invention are at their most favorable. The symphony orchestra favors musical advance officially, but it dare not offer much of it at a time. It must advance slowly, because it deals with a large public, which necessarily is slow of comprehension, and because the basis of its whole operation is the conserving of tradition anyway. Stability rather than variety is what the faithful chiefly demand of it.

Our symphony orchestras, historically viewed, are solider than our banks. They are always getting born; they rarely die. Constantly threatened with financial disaster (a talking point during campaigns to raise money or in union negotiations), they almost never cease operations. Nor will they, so long as civic pride exists and so long as democratic government through parliamentary procedure shall seem to us a beautiful ideal worthy of representation in art.

December 28, 1947

The Delights of Autumn

PHILADELPHIA ORCHESTRA, EUGENE ORMANDY, conductor, first New York concert of the season last night in Carnegie Hall. Soloist, GERTRUDE RIBLA, soprano.

TOCCATA AND FUGUE IN D MINOR	BACH-ORMANDY
SYMPHONY NO. 2, IN D MAJOR, OP. 43	SIBELIUS
THREE FRAGMENTS FROM *Wozzeck,* for voice and orchestra	BERG
Daphnis et Chloë, SUITE NO. 2	RAVEL

The Philadelphia Orchestra opened its New York season last night in Carnegie Hall with a showpiece for the group's justly famous string section, a third-rate symphony correctly supposed to be popular, some excerpts from one of the great dramatic works of our century that is incorrectly supposed to be unpopular simply because our Metropolitan Opera has never produced it, and a standard dessert-piece that is both popular and first-class music. The execution of all these works under the leadership of Eugene Ormandy was a dream of beauty.

Mr. Ormandy's transcription, heard here for the first time, of the Bach Toccata and Fugue in D minor for organ is not limited in its orchestration to the string choir; but it is a showpiece for strings all the same. This arrangement employs only brief moments of woodwind relief and of brass re-enforcement at the climaxes. It makes the strings work practically all the time and mostly alone, displays to advantage all the delicacy and all the power of a string body matchless, to my knowledge, anywhere in the world. With a group of more modest equipment in this regard, the present version might sound poor. For the Philadelphia Orchestra it is just right.

Alban Berg's *Wozzeck,* though familiar in Central European opera houses before the war and celebrated all over the world, has been little given in this country. Whenever it has been produced, even in the form of brief concert excerpts, it has made a profound impression. Last spring Bernard Herrmann played bits of it on the C.B.S. "Invitation to Music" program. Werner Janssen has recorded four sides of it. Publicly, however, the work has not been heard in New York since Leopold Stokowski gave the whole opera here in 1931 for the League of Composers.

That timidity is no longer justified in presenting so simply expressive a work to the public was proved last night by its warm reception. The Sibelius Second Symphony received, along with sustained applause, some boos. The Berg work received only applause, in my hearing, and lots of it. Its instrumental performance, which was a marvel of clarity, was perfectly clear, I think, to all in its direct emotional communication. Vocally Gertrude Ribla got through it, but she could not be said to have done so by the exclusive use of agreeable sounds. It lies a little high for her, as a matter of fact. Also, the work itself is less expressive vocally than instrumentally. But in every way it is deeply moving music and should be heard oftener.

Somehow the idea has got round that this is twelve-tone music and hence hard to understand. It is neither. It is chromatic music of straightforward romantic feeling that should cause no real confusion today, twenty-seven years after its completion. Even if it did, it would still merit more frequent performance than it receives. What are symphony orchestras and opera companies for, after all? Aren't they supposed to educate us, to give us, along with the classics, the best that our time has produced?

The evening ended with a reminder, in the form of Ravel's second *Daphnis et Chloë* suite, that the sound of the Philadelphia Orchestra, indoors, heard again after some months, is one of the dependable delights of autumn.

October 8, 1947

Luminous

PHILADELPHIA ORCHESTRA, PIERRE MONTEUX, conductor, second New York concert of the season last night in Carnegie Hall.

SYMPHONY NO. 7, IN A MAJOR, OP. 92	BEETHOVEN
SYMPHONY NO. 3	WILLEM PIJPER
SYMPHONY IN B FLAT MAJOR	CHAUSSON

Pierre Monteux, conducting the Philadelphia Orchestra last night in Carnegie Hall, produced, I think, the most beautiful orchestral sounds I have ever heard. Throughout the whole dynamic range of which that delicate and powerful group is capable there was not one note of heaviness. All was pure glow and luminosity, loveliness, brightness, and sheer auditory incandescence.

The musical readings of the great San Franciscan were no less passionately lucid than the sounds in which they were embodied. Beethoven's Seventh was ever reposed and alert. The Chausson Symphony was warm of color and rich of contour. Willem Pijper's Third Symphony, played in memory of the composer, who died on March 19 of this year, was a vigorous evocation of a strong spirit and a master workman.

This work, written in 1926, is a period piece from the time when modern music was still uncompromising. Prefaced as an attempt to "move the powers of hell," it exploits the monotony of ostinato, the banality of commercialized dance rhythms, and a general contrariness of harmony and counterpoint with a master's mastery of dissonant effect and with genuinely original invention of surprising sound combinations. Its expressive message, which leans a shade heavily on the tenderness-and-irony of Ravel, is perhaps less original than its instrumentation. That is no doubt the reason for the modesty of Pijper's successes outside his native Holland. The work nevertheless has character and force. It sounds like all the other advanced music of its time, but no other music of the time sounds quite like it. It is arbitrary but not sectarian, harsh but not ugly, minor poetry, if you wish, but far from negligible.

Any work thoroughly characteristic of the 1920's is hard to sell these days. Like yesterday's modernistic furniture made of chromium and pigskin, of rubber, glass, and oriental woods, upholstered in velvets of violet, dark gray, and black, or even in red fur, it seems as outlandish today, as willfully absurd, as late Victorian furnishings, now so fashionable, appeared to the bright spirits of twenty years ago. Time has gone by it, but not yet far enough for the preoccupations of its decade to become for us poetry. They will become so, of course. And when they do, the epoch's works of art that embody them characteristically will take on a new value. Naturally, those that are strongest of construction will survive best our present day's neglect and misunderstanding. A work so solidly, so handsomely built as Willem Pijper's Third Symphony cannot fail, it seems to me, to be highly considered by some later age, perhaps more highly than some of those works of its period that we now consider cardinal. You never can tell, of course; but workmanship and strong materials are a mighty bulwark against moth and rust.

The Chausson Symphony, composed in the 1890's, has occasionally appeared to me a trifle moth-eaten. Not so last night. It, too, is a period piece, out of Schubert and Wagner's *Parsifal* by a pupil of César Franck. But it is warm, deeply sincere, and not at all badly put together, in spite of its school-of-Franck clichés. It has survived the modernist critics of the 1920's, who couldn't see it at all, and has become beautiful again. At least it was wondrously so last night in Pierre Monteux's luminous transfiguration of it. It is too bad that we have access here to Mr. Monteux's transfigurations only once or twice a year. This listener could do with lots more of Mr. Monteux than that.

October 29, 1947

Prince of Impressionism

PHILADELPHIA ORCHESTRA, ERNEST ANSERMET, conductor, last night
in Carnegie Hall.

SYMPHONY NO. 38, IN D MAJOR (K. 504), *Prague*	MOZART
Symphonic Poem, *The Song of the Nightingale*	STRAVINSKY
Orchestral Suite, *Pelléas et Mélisande,* OP. 80	FAURÉ
La Mer, Three Symphonic Sketches	DEBUSSY

Cries of "Bravo!" sounded in Carnegie Hall last night as Ernest
Ansermet, conducting the Philadelphia Orchestra, brought to a
close the final dazzling pages of Debussy's *La Mer.* The whole
concert had been dazzling, indeed, and not through any playing of
tricks on audience psychology or any of the grosser forms of auditory tonal appeal. The great Swiss conductor had held us all enthralled, as he had the orchestra itself, by sheer musicianship, by
knowledge, by understanding, by a care for aural beauty and for
exactitude.

In appearance a simple professor, touched up perhaps toward both
Agamemnon and the King of Clubs, he is at once a sage, a captain,
and a prince. With wisdom, firmness, and grace he rules his domain;
and that domain is the music of Impressionism. For other leaders the
center of the world may be Beethoven or Brahms or Wagner. For
him it is the music of Debussy and all that borders thereon. No
one living, not even Monteux, can command him in that repertory.
Smooth as a seashell, iridescent as fine rain, bright as the taste of
a peach are the blends and balances of orchestral sound with which
he renders, remembering, the lines, the backgrounds, and the tonal
images of the great tonal painters who worked in France round
the turn of our century.

Mozart he plays with love and with light, too; and he began last
night with the *Prague* Symphony, just to show us how a classical
rendering can be clean and thoroughly musical without being dry or
overcrisp. The Philadelphia players found his company on that
ground a privilege and gave of their best, which is the world's best.

But it was only royalty on a visit. With Stravinsky, Fauré, and Debussy the king was back in his land, in his own house reigning, informed, understanding, understood, obeyed from a glance.

Stravinsky's *Song of the Nightingale,* arranged from an opera score and reorchestrated into a symphonic poem in 1919, may well represent this composer at his highest mastery of instrumental evocation. Musically, nevertheless, the work is weak from lack of thematic integration and harmonic structure. It gives pleasure as sound, page by page, palls as musical continuity in the concert room. It needs to be played from time to time because it is a work of the highest and most striking fancy, but heaven preserve us from it as a repertory piece.

Fauré's *Pelléas et Mélisande* suite, on the other hand, is a work of deep loveliness that could stand more usage in repertory than it gets these days. When played with such sweet harmoniousness and such grace of line as it was last night, one wonders why one had forgotten how touching it can be.

Debussy's *The Sea* brought the wonders of the evening to a radiant close. It is a piece this reviewer has always found a shade disappointing; but it is a popular repertory work; and if one has to hear it, Ansermet's reading of it is more welcome than most. Actually, while listening to it, this unfriendly witness forgot all about his prejudices and enjoyed himself thoroughly, almost as thoroughly as during the Mozart and the Fauré.

January 19, 1949

Koussevitzky

Serge Koussevitzky, in devoting recently to American works two whole programs out of the Boston Symphony Orchestra's ten New York concerts of the season, has rendered a service to music and to the public. He has also reminded us of his own assiduous care for living music and for public instruction. Ten years ago, at the end of the fifteenth year of his tenure with that orchestra, he played a comparable series of works, the cream, in his judgment, of those by American authors that he had previously played. This time he has selected from the last ten years of his activity works and authors that mark a decade and that taken together make up another arch in that vast monument to the creative spirit of his time that is this conductor's whole public career.

It is of no importance to note, save in passing, that Mr. Koussevitzky's list of new works and authors is not the complete list of America's distinguished music. Moore, Luening, Wagenaar, and others are conspicuously absent. Sessions appears but once, and not among the revivals. At no time have Ruggles or Varèse, historical figures both, been represented. It is far more valuable to remember that his complete recent lists are more ample than anybody else's (save possibly Manuel Rosenthal's with the French Orchestre National). It is also useful to recall that though he came to this country with a long history of living works played and of composers encouraged, his collaboration with the musical life of his time in America had been facilitated by the similar activities of his predecessor, Pierre Monteux, in Boston, of his younger contemporary, Leopold Stokowski, in Philadelphia, and of the forerunners of them all, Walter Damrosch, in New York, and Frederick Stock, in Chicago. If Serge Koussevitzky has played more new American music than these others, that is largely because in his time there has been more of it to play. Our enlightened leaders have always given us what there was.

Even so, and placing him in the company of all those responsible to history, Mr. Koussevitzky merits an award in this last year of his Boston tenure, an award that history will certainly bestow upon him but that we still living could do honor to ourselves by offering earlier. For no other musical interpreter living has done so much for so many all over the world. As conductor, as publisher, as commissioner of works, he has assumed the music of his time (and it has been a long time) to be worthy of his support, financial, musical, and moral. He has published, played, taught, and paid, spent of his fortune, his earnings, his time, and his vigor without stint. In Russia, in Germany, in France, and in the United States, wherever his life has been led, even for short periods, he has left his mark on music and helped other men of music to leave theirs. His huge personal talent has been devoted to a cause, that cause the inclusion of the living creator, along with the listener, in the life of art.

Had his talent not been so vast, his achievement would have been less remarkable. But even with gifts so grand, the danger of personal aggrandizement is always present. He could so easily, with a lesser consecration, have come to fame without all that labor and expense. He chose otherwise, because he is a man of moral, as well as artistic, responsibility. He could not devote less than all his resources to the art that is his spiritual life. A man of humble origins, he has known that people, the people, means all the people there are and that art must belong to all the people and draw its strength from all the people. Common folk, aristocrats, intellectuals, the moneyed, the musical—it takes them all nowadays to make music make sense. And being a leader, if one's talent imposes such a responsibility, requires a full man's full time.

Koussevitzky has been a full man and given full-time service during a long lifetime. That service, we hope, is far from ended; but his twenty-five years as conductor of the world's most celebrated orchestra are drawing to a close. It is only just that at this time the whole world of music make him aware of its gratitude for services rendered, pay him some outward sign of the deep honor it owes him. Let these words stand as evidence of one musician's appreciation.

January 23, 1949

Wondrous Musical Beauties

CLEVELAND ORCHESTRA, GEORGE SZELL, conductor, last night in Carnegie Hall. Soloist, CLIFFORD CURZON, pianist.

SYMPHONY IN C MAJOR (K. 551), *Jupiter*	MOZART
CONCERTO FOR ORCHESTRA	BARTÓK
PIANO CONCERTO NO. 4, IN G MAJOR, OP. 58	BEETHOVEN

The Cleveland Orchestra, playing last night in Carnegie Hall under the direction of its regular conductor George Szell, gave ·distinguished execution to a distinguished program. Mozart's *Jupiter,* Bartók's Concerto for Orchestra and Beethoven's Fourth Piano Concerto, masterworks all, made no appeal to what we may call the "lower element" in a listener's mind. The latter piece, indeed, as played by Clifford Curzon, brought all our minds, I think, to higher ground than is our concert habitat. The soloist received also, as did Mr. Szell after the Bartók, an ovation hugely larger than it is our New York custom to award.

The beauties of this particular execution came no less from the orchestra than from the solo instrument. Mr. Curzon's vast variety of kinds of tone, his unfailing beauty of sound, his tender grace and grand perspectives of expression all made his rendering both a message and a monument. But Mr. Szell's sensitivity in drawing from his excellent orchestra sounds and curves no less noble, no less constantly fresh and surprising, completed, filled out one of the loveliest musical executions it has been my pleasure to hear in some time.

The other works were read with cleanliness and solid proportions; but a certain foursquareness in the first and last movements of the Mozart symphony and a shade of brutality in the dramatic accents of the Bartók Concerto caused them both to fall short, at least for this listener, of the ultimate elegance. When a leader of lesser refinement progresses as steadily through a Mozart symphony as if he were swimming the Channel, one is grateful for lack of distortion. But when a musician whose musical mind and skill are of the first quality fails to take advantage of every occasion for bringing out metrical contrasts and irregular stresses, one is a little disappointed. One had hoped the streamlining taste in symphonic interpretation had passed from fashion. Certainly no such obviousness marred the performance of the Beethoven Concerto.

The Cleveland Orchestra, long an excellent one, seems to have taken on added musical quality under this conductor. The string section is homogeneous as to color, plays with a mat tone that is dark but never heavy. The vibrato is warm but discreet. The fortissimo is as musical a sound as the pianissimo. The bowing is long, flexible, and subtle. The wind sections are in every way satisfactory, but the strings made a deeper impression on this listener. The Cleveland Orchestra, in fact, seems to him one that bears comparison with the best we know. Certainly its concert last night was full of wondrous musical beauties.

February 15, 1950

Expert and Original

St. Louis Symphony Orchestra, Vladimir Golschmann, conductor, first New York concert last night in Carnegie Hall.

Overture and Allegro	Couperin-Milhaud
Symphony No. 40, in G minor (K. 550)	Mozart
Magic Manhattan	Manuel Rosenthal
(First New York performance)	
Verklärte Nacht, for strings, Op. 4	Schönberg
Dances from *The Three-Cornered Hat*	De Falla

The St. Louis Symphony Orchestra, second oldest organization of the kind in the country, now in its seventieth year, gave its first New York concert last night in Carnegie Hall. A brilliant concert

it was, too, both as to program and to playing. Vladimir Golschmann, now in his twentieth year as conductor of the St. Louis body,
directed with verve and all musical elegance. His orchestra is not
quite the equal of our Eastern Big Three nor, perhaps, even of
Cleveland now nor of Chicago in its best days; but it is an accomplished and well-trained group, sensitive as to nuance and rich of
tone; and Mr. Golschmann is a conductor with life in him as well
as musicianship. His concert was for this reviewer one of the most
delightful of the season.

An Overture and Allegro from the quartet by Couperin known
as *La Sultane*, orchestrated with style and spirit by Darius Milhaud (and similarly executed) began it. Mozart's G-minor Symphony continued its classical portion, played with a manly directness
and also with a greater attention to shading and phraseology than
is nowadays the custom. Schönberg's *Verklärte Nacht*, rendered
with all the passionate romanticism of its author's youth, and three
dances from De Falla's ballet *The Three-Cornered Hat*, played
to the hilt for their Spanish as well as for their theatrical content,
closed it with tenderness and brilliance. The center of it was a brand-
new piece by Manuel Rosenthal.

This work written in 1948 and entitled *Magic Manhattan*, is a
companion piece to Gershwin's *American in Paris*. It represents
a Frenchman's visit to New York. Beginning with a train departure
from the Gare Saint-Lazare, it continues through a first view of
our skyscrapers, the landing pier, a quiet side street or two, Times
Square in full blast, Chinatown, the Bowery, the lower East Side,
and the upper West Side with its majestic Hudson River, to a spectacle of dawn over the city. It is a panorama with breadth in it,
astonishment, and (in the slum scenes) compassion. It is witty,
picturesque, entertaining; but it catches also the violence and the
power of the world's metropolis. Every now and then a passing
elevated train makes its sudden racket and disappears.

As always in the work of this composer, the orchestral score is of
an originality, an accuracy of effect, a virtuosity incomparable. The
note textures, the tunes, and the harmony, though by no means
undistinguished, are perhaps less strikingly inventive than the in-

rumental sounds and combinations. Their quality, and it is an unusual one in music so clearly pictorial, comes from the fact that they are musical at all. Other writers engaging in what might well be taken for pure orchestration make their pieces just that. They produce the right sounds; but their music, as music, is mostly noodling. Mr. Rosenthal's, for all its predominance of color over shape, bears examination and re-hearing. It is interesting as well as fun, sincerely felt, cleanly thought, wholly void of vulgarity.

Magic Manhattan is not easy to situate among today's music. It has a hard core of originality and a purity of communicative intention that remove it from the Hollywood kind. Its lack of multiple meaning, of perspective in the sentiment, keeps it for the present out of official art-music categories. Its closest mate, though the subject of one is humane and of the other spiritual, is Messiaen's *Liturgies of the Divine Presence,* or possibly his *Turangalila.* In both cases an expert engineer has designed a complex musical machine for specific expressivity. In both cases the machine is efficient, the expression clear. In Messiaen's case the aim is more pretentious; in Rosenthal's the result is more fun. In both, France has produced a new kind of music, beautiful, wonderfully expert, and, as always when there is novelty, a little shocking.

March 9, 1950

Musical Horse Show

PHILHARMONIC-SYMPHONY ORCHESTRA, VICTOR DE SABATA, conductor, last night in Carnegie Hall.

OVERTURE to *La Gazza Ladra*	ROSSINI
Symphonie Fantastique	BERLIOZ
Preludio Magico	FRAZZI
(First New York performance)	
SPIRITUALS FOR STRING CHOIR AND ORCHESTRA	GOULD
"Ride of the Valkyries" from *Die Walküre*	WAGNER

Victor De Sabata, if one may believe last night's concert of the Philharmonic, which he conducted, is what used to be called in horsy circles a great whip. Certainly he rode the orchestra hard and well, made it play soft and slow, loud and fast, stop dead in its tracks, change gaits, do everything but spell. He himself spelled out the scores for us clearly, unmistakably. If occasionally, as in the Berlioz *Symphonie Fantastique*, he seemed doubtful of our ability to catch the meaning, or, as in the Morton Gould Spirituals, to have missed it himself, there is no question but that he knew their notes backwards. Surely he is a skilled technician of the *haute école*.

His program, consisting entirely of showpieces, offered as its only rarity a *Preludio Magico* by Vito Frazzi, an Italian professor now in his sixties. This work, composed in the Impressionistic taste and suavely orchestrated, is a civilized piece. It lacks a striking thematic content; but it is agreeable to listen to, with its spicy string-and-wind mixtures of sounds, its clean rhetoric and accomplished workmanship. It would have been even more a pleasure had the conductor not overplayed his brasses in the climax.

He overplayed everything, in fact, to such a degree that what with huge accents, imperceptible pianissimos, interminable pauses, and static slow passages, everything lost cohesion, came out void of line or progress. This kind of musical eagerness-to-hit-us-between-the-eyes could not wholly conceal from us the familiar thought content of Rossini and Berlioz, though it did occasionally bury the sound of the full string body under a brassy canopy. But Mr. De

Sabata's incessant tampering with tempos caused him to miss every trick in playing with Mr. Gould's seemingly simple but far from unsophisticated American metrics. This composer's Spirituals for String Choir and Orchestra, overdressed as it is orchestrally and harmonically, has its own rhythmic life, supports no imposition of any merely theatrical animation. Itself all trickiness, the addition of jugglery from another school plain breaks its back.

Thankfully, deadline considerations made joining Wagner's Valkyries in their Ride inadvisable for the reviewer. One had been carried along by that time on quite enough battle horses. One had admired the skill of the rider but lost confidence in his sense of destination. He had put the orchestra through its paces over and over but not convinced one of a single thing. So much musical skill combined with so little musical taste would surely be of more brilliant effect in the theater than in the concert hall.

March 3, 1950

A Knack for Landscape

PHILHARMONIC-SYMPHONY ORCHESTRA, VICTOR DE SABATA, conductor, last night in Carnegie Hall. Soloist, ARTUR RUBINSTEIN, pianist.

OVERTURE to *I Vespri Siciliani*	VERDI
PIANO CONCERTO IN A MAJOR (K. 488)	MOZART
SYMPHONY NO. 5, IN E MINOR, *From the New World*	DVOŘÁK
RHAPSODY ON A THEME OF PAGANINI	RACHMANINOFF

Victor De Sabata, conducting the Philharmonic last night, revealed an aspect of his mind that had not been strongly in evidence on the previous occasion of this reporter's attendance. I refer to his subtlety in the handling of landscape music. The program opened

18

with a skillful but on the whole claptrap reading of Verdi's overture to *The Sicilian Vespers*. Whether a similar dynamic exaggeration at the expense of line marred his reading at the end, with Artur Rubinstein as piano soloist, of Rachmaninoff's Paganini Variations the lateness of the hour forbade my knowing, though the work is surely temptation to that for a conductor bent toward that. Nothing of the kind, however, marred the Mozart Piano Concerto in A major or the Dvořák *New World* Symphony.

The former was played straightforwardly and neatly by both soloist and conductor. If it lacked brilliance in the piano part, delicacy was nowhere absent from the accompaniment. Mr. Rubinstein did not make ugly sounds, but he used weight crescendos that are more expressive in the Romantic repertory than in classical works. On the whole, the concerto sounded gray and a shade ineffectual; and I think the soloist is more to be blamed for that effect than the conductor. Mr. Rubinstein was respectful of shape and detail; but he made the work sound small, very small.

Dvořák's *New World* Symphony received from Mr. De Sabata a reading thoroughly live and fresh. Making no effort to confound this with the music of oratory and personal passion, as so many do, he gave it to us very simply as the work of a European landscape painter charmed by American subjects. He even restrained the lyric outpouring of woodwind soloists, kept the whole a picture. It was rich in color, vibrant, full of light in the climaxes, everywhere atmospheric, pastoral, an outdoor piece. Hearing so hackneyed a work sound fresh and new was a pleasure, because the work is intrinsically tender and imaginative. It kept its distance, spoke in poetry, penetrated the spirit in spite of familiarity.

The technical methods by which this effect was achieved were the whole gamut of orchestral fine adjustments and balances that mark the work of skilled conductors. But the poetic idea behind the interpretation was proof of other qualities in Mr. De Sabata, of an intellectual distinction, a refined musical imagination far more in keeping with his European repute than any reading had indicated at his first concert in this city.

March 24, 1950

France at Its Best

French orchestras are the best in the world when they are good and the worst when they are not. Last Sunday's concert of the Orchestre National gave us France's (and probably Europe's) best orchestra playing in a way the present writer has rarely heard the same group do at home. The result was an ultimate in musical delight. But lest any (and they are many) who have been shocked and disappointed, visiting Paris, at run-of-the-mill French orchestral execution, let me explain a little of what really goes on.

Paris has at present five major orchestras besides those of the two chief opera houses. Four of these—the Conservatory, the Colonne, the Lamoureux, and the Pasdeloup—are musicians' co-operatives. They hire their own manager and conductor and share receipts. The two opera orchestras and the fifth symphonic group, l'Orchestre National de la Radiodiffusion Française, are employed by the government; and their members are civil servants. They are paid a modest wage the year round and work eleven months. Since a steady wage is preferable to problematic profits, appointments to these orchestras are sought after. The only group that approaches them in breadwinning power is the Conservatory Orchestra, which gets considerable outside work recording for films. Vacancies in the personnel of all the orchestras are filled by open competitive auditions. Conductors' and soloists' fees are not high.

On account of the low salaries paid and low profits shared, French orchestral players have long been accustomed to accept outside engagements and sent their substitutes to any concert or rehearsal. This substitution privilege makes for undependability in performance. When the National was reorganized after the Liberation by two composers—Henry Barraud, musical director of the French Radio, and Manuel Rosenthal, conductor—the substitute system was abolished in the National Radio Orchestra. Top salaries as French salaries go, and the assured presence of the true personnel at all rehearsals and concerts enabled Barraud and Rosenthal to make of the National an absolutely first-class orchestra. Also, re-

authority. Russians have taken his Moussorgsky and his Korsakov, Italians his Verdi and his Rossini right into the body of their tradition. The present writer is witness that when he plays American music he plays it right.

Beecham's interpretative and technical skills are available at their highest in that most modern branch of the executant's art, gramophone recording. To tell the truth, Sir Thomas is not always at his best in the concert hall. When he is in form, there is nobody so live, so loving, so gracious, so powerful, so perfect. But sometimes he gets overexcited, falls short by his own standards of grandeur and refinement. Not so in the recording studio. There he works in calm, rehearsing, playing back, retaking each record side over and over till every sound in it is a musical sound and contributes to the whole piece's meaningful design. The result is a body of recorded music unequaled by that of any other conductor for either size or quality. The Beecham records have become known round the world both as authoritative musical renderings and as the very definition of good recording.

Four years ago, at the age of sixty-six, Sir Thomas organized a new orchestra, the Royal Philharmonic, trained it, perfected it in the concert hall, began making disks with it for the H. M. V. company ("His Master's Voice"), under the new full frequency recording range ("ffrr") now employed in England. America has received his *Messiah, Electra,* and divers symphonic releases, all excellent. The R. C. A.-Victor Company is now releasing here, as part of the birthday honors, his version (complete) of Gounod's *Faust,* made in London two years ago with the assistance of an all-French cast from the Paris Opera. I heard the test-pressings of this set last year and recommend the album highly. Indeed, my impression from one hearing is that Sir Thomas has again made both musical and recording history, as he did back in 1936 with his recording of Mozart's *Magic Flute* with the Berlin Philharmonic Orchestra and singers from the Berlin Opera.

Considering his excellent health and undiminished vigor, we may hope (d. v.) for a great many more fine concerts and recordings from Sir Thomas, as his enemies may also look for lots more trouble from him, and for a long time. His quarrels, his lawsuits, his indiscreet public addresses are signs of that vigor, its overflow. But the vigor itself is in the music he makes, in the deep humane culture of his mind, in the warmth of his sentiments, in the liveliness of his wit and spirits, in the huge and undaunted devotion of a great man and a grand seigneur to all that music means, ever did, ever will, or ever could mean in the life of a great people.

The English aristocracy, notoriously unmusical, is afraid of him, disapproves of him, calls him "Beecham." America, suspicious and a little resentful of harsh words but respectful all the same, calls him "Sir Thomas." In Britain the plain, common people, who have followed his career for fifty years and know him for a friend, speak of him as "Tommie." But whether in love, respect, healthy fear, or all three sentiments, the English-speaking world has reason to honor and to thank this great man for restoring us all to music's great tradition.

May 8, 1949

Children's Voices

THE LITTLE SINGERS OF PARIS (Les Petits Chanteurs à la Croix de Bois), L'ABBÉ MAILLET, conductor, Saturday night in Carnegie Hall.

Sur le Pont d'Avignon	arr. PERISSAS
Le Chant des Oiseaux (16th Century)	JANNEQUIN
Répands, charmante nuit (17th Century)	LULLY
La Nuit	RAMEAU
Cradle Song	MOZART
Malbrough s'en va-t-en guerre (arr. for double quartet)	D'INDY
L'Alouette	arr. LOTH
Descende in hortum	FEVIN
Tenebrae factae sunt	POULENC
Les deux Cités (cantata in three parts)	MILHAUD
Il est né le Divin Enfant	arr. NOYON
My Bonnie Lies Over the Ocean	arr. KENNET

26

Le Petit Quinquin	arr. Delsinne
Solveig's Song	Grieg
Frère Jacques	arr. de Rause
National Hymns	

"The Little Singers of Paris" (or "La Manécanterie des Petits Chanteurs à la Croix de Bois") gave a concert of unaccompanied vocal music, sacred and secular, last Saturday night in Carnegie Hall. Founded some twenty years ago by their present conductor, the Abbé Maillet, the group is made up of underprivileged slum children, the Parisian equivalent of what we call here "dead-end kids." From a social point of view the enterprise, which is self-supporting, is in every way admirable. From a purely musical one it has, too, many excellences; and its faults, which are few, are only those inherent to the set-up.

The gravest of these is a lack of tonal balance. The basses and tenors are too few, and these are all young adults only recently boy singers in the choir. Their voices are neither strong enough nor resonant enough to support adequately the penetrating brilliance of the sopranos. Even the altos, as is common in boy choirs, are weak compared to the higher voices. As a result, the whole tonal fabric, though piercingly beautiful at times, is top-heavy.

Another disadvantage lies in the musical personality of the choir's founder and director. The Abbé Maillet, though a first-class technician in the training of child voices, a schooled musician, an incomparable animator and executive, is not an interpreter invariably of the highest taste. His program the other evening was overweighted with choral arrangements of familiar melodies and disappointingly skimpy in its attention to the grander reaches of liturgical repertory. His renderings of the lighter numbers, moreover, were marred by overdone comic effects and a lack of sustained rhythm more appropriate to the vaudeville stage than to the concert hall.

On the other hand, he did give us two first-class modern works in serious vein, both written for the Little Singers, a *Tenebrae factae sunt* of Francis Poulenc and Darius Milhaud's cantata in three movements, *Les Deux Cités*. The latter was last sung here,

I believe, by the Collegiate Chorale in 1942 at a Serenade Concert in the Museum of Modern Art. Both are noble works, and both might well prove difficult of execution by an adult professional choir. Well-nigh perfectly intoned by the Little Singers, they gave proof of the choir's sound musical training, of that mastery of rhythm and interval that is the glory of French choral singing today. Throughout the evening, indeed, the boys took in their stride vocal and harmonic difficulties that our own boy choirs are rarely required to hurdle, much less to consider as normal.

A sheer delight were certain soprano voices in solo passages and all the altos singing together. These last had the coppery tinge of violas. The soprano soloists came out like hitherto unheard woodwinds, sailing up to high C with the utmost of naturalness and ease. The whole choir humming gave out a sound as of the most velvet-toned string orchestra. At no point did the boys try to sing like women. They sang in the masque, or upper part of the face, as trained singers should; and their sound was that of true child voices, reedy, rich, sweet, inhuman, disembodied. The experience of this sound, made further nasal and oboelike by a frank intoning of the French vowels, is only to be met with in French child-singing. Heard at its best, as in the work of the Abbé Maillet's Little Singers, it is an experience unforgettable, literally out of this world. It is too bad that the Abbé does not have available to him some mature French tenors and basses and perhaps one adult male alto, singing falsetto, to give body to the lower child voices. The result would certainly be, in the great classic religious repertory, as deeply satisfying as the sound of his present choir is thrilling.

I have dwelt on the sound of the Little Singers because that is unique. It would not be fair to close, however, without mention of their appearance, which is indeed an attractive one. Whether in dark blue street suits with white socks or in their religious robes of white cotton ornamented by a plain wooden cross, they are in every way straightforward and charming. The Abbé is something of a comedian and an inveterate between-courses speaker, but the children are as unpretentious as their singing is beautiful.

October 13, 1947

II. RECITALISTS

King of Pianists

ARTUR RUBINSTEIN, pianist, recital last night in Carnegie Hall.

SONATA IN B MINOR, OP. 58	CHOPIN
Fantasiestücke, OP. 12	SCHUMANN
El Albaicin; Triana	ALBÉNIZ
FOUR MAZURKAS	SZYMANOWSKI
Valse Oubliée; RHAPSODY No. 12	LISZT

Artur Rubinstein, who played a recital of piano music last night in Carnegie Hall, made his first American appearance more than forty years ago. He has long been a great musician and a grand executant; and now, approaching sixty, he is king of his profession.

Others may be regularly more flashy, though few can dazzle so dependably; and none can match him for power and refinement. He plays very loudly and very beautifully, very softly and thoroughly clean, straightforwardly, elegantly, and with a care for both the amenities of musical discourse and the clear transmission of musical thought. He is a master pianist and a master musician. There has not been his like since Busoni.

The program last night was standard but choice. There were a Chopin sonata (the opus 58), all eight of Schumann's *Fantasiestücke*, two Spanish evocations by Albéniz, four Szymanowski mazurkas, Liszt's exquisite *Valse Oubliée* and Twelfth Rhapsody. There is no point in searching especial excellences of interpretation, for all the works were read, as they were executed, to perfection. Perhaps the Liszt Rhapsody was most striking to this listener for the way Rubinstein made a modern pianoforte sound like a Hungarian zembalom and even like a whole orchestra of them. Perhaps the simplicity of Schumann's *Warum?* merits note, too, the way poetry was here achieved by not insisting on it.

As a matter of fact, Rubinstein builds his huge climactic effects, the most impressive that exist today in piano playing, by "throwing away," as theater people put it, nine-tenths, at least, of his lines. He does not obscure a minor turn or cadence, but neither does he lean on it. He treats it casually and gets on to the main thing. I should not be willing to call his manner of moving through a piece streamlined. It is too deeply aware for that. But the longest and loosest works, under his fingers, do get themselves organized and move forward.

A major device to this end is the lack of all technical hesitancy in sweeping through difficult passages, in keeping their speed, however fast, a function of the whole melodic line and harmonic rhythm. In this respect he is not unique; there are a few other masters who do the same thing. In his handling of transitions, however, in getting from a fast passage into a slow one, in moving from one expressive range to another, he is alone. It is hard to know just how he does it so gracefully, because the new theme has always begun before one has quite noticed. I think, though, that his transitions are operated a little more quickly than is customary. They are not brusque, but he does not hold them back. He moves through them as smoothly as a Diesel locomotive moves in and out of a railway station.

The Szymanowski mazurkas, dedicated to the pianist, are melodious, lacy, charming, and, to this reviewer, disappointing. I suspect that after Chopin, the concert mazurka could benefit more from a return to naturalistic treatment than from efforts at further fanciness. Szymanowski's examples seem to me finicky and overembroidered as folklore evocations.

February 14, 1949

Dramatizing the Structure

CLIFFORD CURZON, pianist, recital yesterday afternoon in Town Hall.

SONATA IN C MINOR (K. 457)	MOZART
SONATA IN D MAJOR, OP. 53	SCHUBERT
FANTASY IN C MAJOR, OP. 17	SCHUMANN

Clifford Curzon, who played yesterday afternoon in the Town Hall, is far and away the most satisfactory interpreter I know of the pianoforte's Romantic repertory. Horowitz may play Liszt with a more diabolic incandescence, and anybody can fancy himself a specialist of Chopin. But Schubert and Schumann are composers whom almost nobody plays convincingly any more. Certainly no one brings them to life with quite the delicacy and the grandeur of Mr. Curzon.

He prefaced them yesterday afternoon with a Mozart sonata, as if to show us how his special treatment of the Romantics had been arrived at. If I understand correctly, he has approached them not so much with a romantic feeling about them as with a taste for classic rhythmic and dynamic layouts. His Mozart sonata (the G minor K. 457) was treated as a symphony. Huge varieties of shortness in the articulation of notes, of color in the sound, of loudness levels sharply differentiated gave it the variety and the proportions of an orchestral score. Metrical steadiness without the imposition of any regular downbeat gave freedom to the Mozart stresses (as written), gave rhythmic perspective and objectivity to the musical shape. He exposed the work as a wide and solid building, made no effort to use it for personal meditation.

The Schubert Sonata in D, opus 53, a far wider and more personally conceived structure, he walked around in. He did not get lost in it or allow us to forget its plan, but he did take us with him to the windows and show us all its sweet and dreaming views of the Austrian countryside, some of them filled with dancing folk. The terraced dynamics and the abstention from downbeat pulsations, just as in the Mozart piece, kept the rendering impersonal at no loss to expressivity. On the contrary, indeed, the dramatization of it as a form, the scaling of its musical elements gave it evocative power as well as grandeur of proportion. And its enormous variety in the kinds of sound employed, its solid basses, and a dry clarity in the materials of its structural filling prevented monotony from becoming a concomitant of its vastness.

With the Schumann Fantasy in C, a work of intense personal lyricism and very little shape at all, Mr. Curzon's objective, orchestral approach turned out, surprisingly, to be just what was needed. It interfered at no point with eloquence or poetry. It merely held the piece together, gave it a color gamut, provided a solid setting and a rich frame for the passionate feelings that are its subject. Again the impersonal, the dramatic approach gave power to the work and breadth to its communication. By sacrificing all improvisatory, all minor-poetry attitudes, he gave us the piece as a large composition and as great poetry. Surely Schumann himself, in composing his personal intensities into a large form, however loosely this is held together, must have had something comparable in mind.

January 8, 1950

Modern Piano Playing

YVONNE LÉFÉBURE, pianist, American debut recital yesterday afternoon in Town Hall.

FANTASIA IN D MINOR (K. 397)	MOZART
PRELUDE AND FUGUE IN A MINOR	BACH-LISZT
SONATA IN A FLAT MAJOR, OP. 110	BEETHOVEN
Trois Images: Reflets dans l'eau, Hommage	
à Rameau, Mouvement	DEBUSSY
NOCTURNE No. 13, OP. 119; BARCAROLLE No. 6, OP. 70	FAURÉ
Le Tombeau de Couperin	RAVEL

Yvonne Léfébure, who played a piano recital yesterday in the Town Hall, is France's top-ranking pianist among those hitherto unheard in this country. At once a technical and a musical master, she belongs in the glorious company of Pierre Fournier, Francis Poulenc, Pierre Bernac, the musicians of the Quatuor Loewenguth and those of the Orchestre National, all of whom have given to our fall season examples of the very best contemporary musical workmanship.

In a program marked throughout its execution by intelligence, musicianship, sensitivity, and solid brilliance, Miss Léfébure's playing of Liszt's transcription of Bach's great A minor organ fugue and of Debussy's rarely played *Images* stood out as unusual experiences for this listener. Her Mozart was sound; her *Tombeau de Couperin* of Ravel was distinguished, her Beethoven Sonata (opus 110) first-class; and her Fauré was perfect. Her Bach and her Debussy seemed to your reviewer a sort of ultimate in both sense and sensibility. Also in the evocation by pianistic means of the quality and color of other instruments.

This orchestrating, so to speak, of the literature of the piano is the specific approach to piano playing that differentiates our century's practice of the art from that of its immediate predecessor; and modern piano music, of course, has mostly been composed with that approach in mind. Debussy, Ravel, and their followers are of orchestral evocation wholly conceived. So also, I am convinced, is

Mozart's piano writing; and so certainly, in terms of the organ, are Liszt's arrangements of Bach.

Modern piano technique exploits, for the purpose of suggesting a great variety of kinds of sound, a great variety of kinds and heights of touch. One of Miss Léfébure's most impressive achievements as a technician is the accuracy with which she can strike whole chords from a height of fifteen inches above the keyboard, strike them with perfect note-balance and agreeable tone at any speed and at any degree of loudness or softness. Her differentiations between time and accent also aid orchestral evocation, because melodic passages, as on the *bel canto* instruments, are played without downbeat stresses, the accentual pattern being rendered, as in real orchestral playing, by sharp pings, deep bell strokes, and articulations recalling those of harp, bow-heel, and the orchestra's percussion group.

This kind of piano playing is far from unfamiliar to us, though our own pianists do not do it so well, on the whole, as the French do. What makes Miss Léfébure's work so thoroughly exciting and fresh are the soundness and the penetrating nature of her musical mind, the rightness of her rhythmic instincts, and the breadth of her musical conceptions. There is fecund drama, too, between the strength of her temperament and the discipline of her preparation. She catches flame but does not burn up. She is at all times spontaneous, but she never improvises a reading. She is a first-class pianist, a first-class musician, and an artist. She is of our time, moreover, even playing Bach.

November 15, 1948

Fulfillment Experienced

WEBSTER AITKEN, pianist, recital last night in Town Hall.

TWO SONATAS, in E MAJOR and D MAJOR	SCARLATTI
FOUR TRANSCRIPTIONS FROM *Emerson* (1920)	IVES
PIANO SONATA	CARTER
RICERCARE AND TOCCATA	MENOTTI
(First New York performance)	
SONATA IN C MINOR, OP. 111	BEETHOVEN

Webster Aitken played last night in the Town Hall one of his most rewarding recitals of piano music. The program, as is so often the case with this artist, was a severe one. A lesser technical and musical master could hardly have got through it, much less held the absorbed attention of his audience. But Mr. Aitken left us all, I think, with a feeling of fulfillment. It is not often in the concert hall that one experiences so deep a satisfaction.

Save for the Scarlatti sonatas, that served for little more than to warm up the pianist's hands and to quiet the audience, everything was thoroughly rendered and thoroughly communicated. Charles Ives's Four Transcriptions from *Emerson*, dated 1920, is a normal-length piano sonata fashioned by its author out of the first movement of his vaster *Concord* Sonata. Like all of Ives's music, it is fascinating harmonically but not very personal in expression: and rhythmically it is a little dead. It is a polyharmonic evocation of German Late Romanticism rather than, to my perception, a portrait of its subject. It can scarcely be a portrait of Mr. Ives's feelings about his subject, either, since its emotional content is all too familiar in other, and many other, contexts. Its chief originality is its chord structure, which is both consistent and interesting. I doubt if it will ever be a very useful repertory piece, for all its airs of grandeur. It is, as expression, too banal.

Elliott Carter's Piano Sonata, written in 1945 and '46, might just possibly be a work for the repertory. This is a sustained piece full of power and brilliance. Its relatively quiet moments, though a shade reminiscent of both Copland and Stravinsky, are not entirely, in feeling, derivative; and as figuration they are quite personal. The brilliant toccatalike passages, of which there are many, are to my ear completely original. I have never heard the sound of them or felt the feeling of them before. They are most impressive indeed. The whole work is serious and not superficial. It would be a pleasure to hear it again, and soon.

Gian-Carlo Menotti's Ricercare and Toccata, composed in 1942 but not previously heard in New York, is perhaps a bit superficial, compared to the Carter sonata. But it is so brilliant, so cheerful and generally pleasant that one was grateful for its presence, along with the Scarlatti pieces, on a program of more weighty works. The chromatic Ricercare, in fact, was melodically most graceful. This listener would have liked it to go on a little longer.

The evening ended not with light fare but with Beethoven's Sonata, Opus 111, no less. Here Mr. Aitken gave a reading not at all traditional but one restudied in the light of tradition. He did not moon over the easy slow passages or slow up for the hard fast ones, as is customary. He gave the whole a rhythmic structure and an emotional progress. If one regretted slightly at moments its relentlessly metallic coloration, one was grateful at all times for the clarity and the force of his transcendent execution. Also for his real Beethoven culture. The piece sounded a little hard, but we are told Beethoven played like that. And its hardness was of crystal and granite, not that of stale Christmas cookies. Mr. Aitken is the most masterful of all our American pianists, and his musical culture is the equal of anybody's from anywhere.

March 13, 1948

Thoroughly Contemporary

EUGENE ISTOMIN, pianist, recital last night in Carnegie Hall.

SONATA QUASI UNA FANTASIA, OP. 27, No. 2	BEETHOVEN
ELEVEN PRELUDES (NOS. 14 to 24)	CHOPIN
TWO PRELUDES: E FLAT MAJOR, OP. 23; A MINOR, OP. 32	RACHMANINOFF
La Fille aux cheveux de lin	DEBUSSY
VARIATIONS ON THE NAME *Abegg*, OP. 1	SCHUMANN
Gaspard de la Nuit	RAVEL

Eugene Istomin, who played a recital of piano music last night in Carnegie Hall, is a schooled technician, a natural musician, and a very young man. The first two advantages keep his work interesting and alive. The other state gives it a certain immaturity that weakens from time to time its expressive tension.

Like many another young person of today, he is not at his best in Romantic repertory. He respects it, plays it with what grace and sentiment he can muster; but he cannot really keep his mind on it. Only the music of his own century draws forth his full mental powers. Just as most of the older pianists, especially those brought up away from the centers of contemporary creation, fake their moderns, when they play them at all, so Mr. Istomin is obliged to fake his Romantics—his Schumann, his Chopin, and his Beethoven. The former's *Abegg* Variations he got through on sheer virtuosity. But his Chopin Preludes and his *Moonlight* Sonata were the work of a skillful and gifted child, nothing more.

Even two Preludes of Rachmaninoff and one by Debussy were read with more plain animal warmth than imaginative penetration. It was Ravel who brought out the young man's full expressive powers. The latter's triptych, *Gaspard de la Nuit,* which has tripped up both technically and expressively many a mature master, was just homework to this gifted youth. He played this intricate and difficult work so cleanly, so delicately, so powerfully, with such variety and beauty of touch, such easy understanding of its sense and motivations, with such command and such sincerity that it is impossible, on the basis of that rendering alone, to deny him recognition as an artist of the highest possibilities.

It is not fair to ask the young people of today, simply because they are in accord with their time, to drop the Romantic repertory and the Classical sonatas. The whole of music is their province, and they must get to know it as best they can. All the same, the modern world is where they live and feel at home. Their dealings with Romanticism are a child's version of an old wives' tale, or a city boy's dream of the Far West. They are Romanticism's drugstore cowboys, or at best college students who know the heroic days out of books and photographs. But they do know their time, love it, and take it for eternal, just as the Romantics did theirs. That is why they can make beauty of its masterpieces. That part of their work is real and thoroughly grand. The rest is just culture. And it is on the whole healthier for art that the contemporary in spirit should be authentic and the revivals of past time a product of intellectual ingenuity than that the reverse should obtain. Mr. Istomin is, in this sense, a healthy spirit as well as a good musician.

February 21, 1948

Beauty, Distinction, Mastery

NATHAN MILSTEIN, violinist, recital last night in Carnegie Hall. Assisting pianist, ARTHUR BALSAM.

ADAGIO AND RONDO	STAMITZ
PARTITA IN D MINOR (violin alone)	BACH
SONATA IN G MAJOR, OP. 30, No. 3	BEETHOVEN
CAPRICES IN E FLAT, No. 17, and G MINOR, No. 16 (violin alone)	PAGANINI
Russian Maiden's Song	STRAVINSKY-DUSHKIN
Berceuse sur le nom de Fauré	RAVEL
INTRODUZIONE ED ALLEGRO	NABOKOV

(First performance)

Nathan Milstein gave last night in Carnegie Hall one of the most delightful evenings of violin music that your announcer has experienced in some time. Long suspicious of nationally advertised brands in violin playing, this writer had never before attended a recital by Mr. Milstein, though occasional concertos heard in orchestral concerts had prepared him for full technical satisfaction and pretty sounds. But you can never tell from a concerto what an artist's personality is like and whether he has a banal or an interesting communication to make with his technical skill.

Mr. Milstein, in the opinion of this reporter, is one of the most distinguished musicians now playing the violin in public. He has a cool mat tone, and he does not force it. He has an impeccable left hand technique and a bow arm that never takes anything the easy way if another is more beautiful. His phrase is long, sustained without heaviness, turned with a natural grace. His musical understanding is broad, his personal presentation both authoritative and modest.

The most notable musical achievement of the evening was his performance of the Bach D minor Partita, for violin alone, that lasted nigh on to a half hour and that was sheer heaven from beginning to end for beauty of tone and all round musical lucidity. A work ordinarily considered difficult for audiences was projected with full clarity and with a consistent loveliness that provoked the kind of applause that the press used to call an ovation and that last night caused Mr. Milstein to interrupt his program by the insertion of an encore (a Bach Gigue, I think it was).

Beethoven's G major Sonata, Opus 30, No. 3, was played, with Arthur Balsam at the piano, no less lavishly. The rapid passages were light as wind, airy and dry and insubstantial. The cantilena was poetic without insistence, the whole a triumph of taste and of delicate understanding. Mr. Balsam's work throughout was a musical contribution not to be dismissed with the term accompaniment.

The novelties of the evening were an Adagio and Rondo of Stamitz, played at the beginning, and an Introduction and Allegro of Nicholas Nabokov (a first performance), played at the end. The first was melodious and graceful enough to explain Mozart's admiration of this composer. The second had a quality of personal poetry all too rare in these days of knock-'em-out neo-Classicism. It is a neo-Romantic piece rather than a neo-Classic one, because it is about its subject, not its form, and because that subject is personal feelings. These seem, from the melodic conformation, to be connected with Russia—a wistful sadness, a moment of exuberance, and a return to the wistful note. It is thin writing, widely spaced by moments and always conceived as a blend of piano and violin sound. It is brilliant, too, an original and effective piece of music. Coming at the end of the program, it crowned charmingly an evening of serious and sincere music making, left no taste of condescension or of that relaxing of the musical standards so common at the end of recital programs.

November 18, 1947

Violence and Virtuosity

ERICA MORINI, violinist, recital last night in Carnegie Hall. Assisting pianist, LEON POMMERS.

LARGHETTO	HANDEL
SONATA	VIVALDI-RESPIGHI
CHACONNE (violin alone)	BACH
VIOLIN CONCERTO NO. 5	WIENIAWSKI
SONATA IN D, OP. 11, No. 2	HINDEMITH
THREE FANTASTIC DANCES	SHOSTAKOVITCH
INVOCATION AND DANCE	LEO NADELMANN

(First performance)

Erica Morini, if one can judge from her last night's recital in Carnegie Hall, is a violinist of transcendent technical equipment with an especial gift for brio. She plays so handsomely as to pitch and sound and with such dramatic impact as to rhythm that one is tempted, at the beginning, to throw the metaphorical hat in air and shout to oneself, "This is it!" Nevertheless, after a bit, the mind begins to wander. By intermission time it is saying to itself, "What's wrong with this?" By the end of the evening one knows that the musical conceptions of this otherwise deeply impressive artist have all been superficial.

They were superficial last night because they were all based on violent contrasts of volume from one phrase to another, even, occasionally, within a single phrase. This kind of expression is appropriate to some music. The Wieniawski Concerto and Shostakovitch's Fantastic Dances take it admirably, especially if the technique of the executant, as in Miss Morini's case, is solid enough not to explode under its stress. It does not do much, though, for Handel and Bach and Vivaldi. And it is the last thing in the world for plumbing the rich depths of Hindemith's Sonata in D, Op. II, No. 2.

This last, a work of its author's romantic youth, is both melodious and massive. It stems architecturally from Brahms and soars like Fauré. It is a grand piece and a difficult one. Miss Morini, not fazed in the least by its technical difficulties, gave it a serious and certainly a reflected reading. But her preoccupation seemed to be chiefly one of making it sweep along, rather than of allowing it full expressive articulation in its progress. The work is a pleasure to hear, because one hears it seldom. But one regretted that Miss Morini, for all her good will toward it and serious intentions, did not seem to feel as comfortable with it as she obviously did with the Wieniawski.

Perhaps the Wieniawski Concerto is her piece, or her kind of piece. Perhaps, also, on other occasions she can be convincing in other kinds of pieces. Last night your reporter suspected that she would always be at her best in works that it is legitimate to conceive as vehicles for violence and virtuosity. Certainly she was handsome in those.

November 29, 1947

Virtuoso Makes Music

PIERRE FOURNIER, cellist, American debut recital yesterday afternoon in Town Hall. Assisting pianist, GEORGE REEVES.

CHORALE, *Nun kommt der Heiden Heiland*	BACH
SUITE NO. 6, IN D MAJOR	BACH
SONATA NO. 2, IN F MAJOR	BRAHMS
SONATA	DEBUSSY
SONATA	LOCATELLI
VARIATIONS FOR ONE STRING	PAGANINI

Pierre Fournier, who played a cello recital yesterday afternoon in the Town Hall, is at the top of a profession in which skill runs high these days, especially in France. I do not know his superior among living cellists, and there are few who can equal him either for technical mastery or for musical taste. Some play louder, many exploit a more obvious sentiment. I do not know any who give one more profoundly the feeling of having been present at music making.

Excellence in the technical handling of the cello is always primarily a matter of avoiding pitfalls. Mr. Fournier does not let his instrument groan or scratch or squeak or buzz, and yesterday he did not miss exact pitch on more than just a very few notes. Neither did he at any time force his tone beyond the volume of optimum sonority. His sound, in consequence, was always pleasant and, thanks to Mr. Fournier's fine musical sensitivity, extremely varied.

That sensitivity was present in positive form, moreover, as liveness of rhythm and in the wonderful shaping and shading of each line and phrase. Many cellists can play with dignity and style, as Mr. Fournier did, an unaccompanied Bach suite; but few can play a Brahms sonata, as he did yesterday the F major, with such buoyancy and spontaneity, such grace of feeling and no heaviness at all. I know of none who can match him in the Debussy Sonata.

This work is rather a rhapsody than a sonata in the classical sense, and yet it needs in execution a sonata's continuous flow and long-line planning. It needs also the utmost of delicacy and of variety in coloration and a feeling of freedom in its rhythmic progress. Its performance yesterday by Mr. Fournier and his accompanist, George Reeves, was a high point in a season already notable for good ensemble work and a summit capable of dominating many, as regards the rendering of this particular piece.

A master's program such as Mr. Fournier gave us would have been incomplete without a work from the cello's classical period; and there was one, a sonata by Locatelli, noble, charming, and brilliant. The closing piece was a transcription from Paganini, originally written, I think, for the violin's G string, in this version played on the A string of the cello. It is a set of variations on a tender theme of Victorian cast, not a work of marked musical invention but one rich of fancy as regards technical figuration. Its well-nigh impeccable execution brought forth applause of a kind every artist loves to hear. In this case I am sure it was a tribute not only to a virtuoso's prowess but also to his taste and musicianship.

November 14, 1948

Brilliant and Diffuse

GREGOR PIATIGORSKY, cellist, recital last night in Carnegie Hall. Assisting pianist, RALPH BERKOWITZ.

SONATA IN C MAJOR	BOCCHERINI
PRELUDE AND FUGUE IN C MINOR (from Fifth Suite for cello alone)	BACH
SONATA IN G MINOR, OP. 65	CHOPIN
SONATA	DEBUSSY
Elégie	FAURÉ
ARIA	STRAVINSKY
VARIATIONS ON A PAGANINI THEME	PIATIGORSKY

Gregor Piatigorsky, our most popular touring cellist, played to a large audience last night in Carnegie Hall. He played a distinguished program and was more than warmly received. The soloist's execution was brilliant and his accompanist, when audible, excellent. And yet somehow the evening was not quite a first-class musical occasion.

The trouble seems to be that Mr. Piatigorsky is more expert than imaginative. He is a virtuoso in the old style. He has a huge sound, huge hands to reach about the cello's fingerboard with, and a vast variety of tone color. His musical sense is a cultivated one, too. He would seem to have everything. Everything, at least, but concentrated thought. He rarely keeps to the same mood for fifteen seconds. In the midst of a smooth cantilena like that of the Fauré *Elégie* he suddenly introduces the biting-bow declamatory style. To the sustained and interior poetry of the Debussy Sonata he adds an oratorical crescendo, returns to the poetry, then pushes his bow into more crescendo, plays handsomely in duet with the piano in the pizzicato passages, then utters a phrase of interlocked harmony with the pianoforte as if he were all alone on the stage. He plays one phrase like an angel and then scratches the next as only a six-footer with a long bow-arm can scratch. He makes beautiful sounds and ugly sounds, complete sense and no sense, fine music and commonplace music all in one piece, in any piece. His talent and

44

mastery are tops; but he does not seem always to have his mind, though it apparently is a good one, on what he is doing.

From the Boccherini Sonata in C major through the Prelude and Fugue of the Bach C minor ("Discordable") Suite (played in normal tuning), the Chopin Sonata, and the Debussy Sonata to the final oddments, not one piece was read with sustained expressive power; and yet not one reading was without its commanding traits. An enormous competence and a certain indifference marked them all. In spite of a receptive audience, the artist seemed unable to call forth that concentrated attention on his own work that is, if not the whole state of inspired artistry, its sine qua non.

Perhaps your reporter is lending his own incomplete attention to the proceedings to a sincere and hard-working soloist. He hopes not. And he thinks not, since he is ascribing to the artist not lethargy so much as a nervous, almost a mercurial discontinuity of thought. If that were of a continuous intensity, Piatigorsky would be continuously fascinating. As it is, or as it was last night, this listener found him both fascinating and tedious, impressive and banal all at once.

March 20, 1948

A Major Experience

MARTIAL SINGHER, baritone, recital yesterday afternoon in Town Hall. Assisting pianist, PAUL ULANOWSKY.

"My Heart Now is Merry," from *Phoebus and Pan*	BACH
AIR OF THESEUS, from *Hippolyte et Aricie*	RAMEAU
"Che faro senza Euridice," from *Orfeo*	GLUCK
Three *Etudes Latines: Lyde, Tyndaris, Phyllis;*	
Les Cygnes; La Pêche	REYNALDO HAHN
Jota; FINALE from *El Retablo de Maese Pedrell*	MANUEL DE FALLA
Chansons Madécasses: Nahandova; Aouah; Il est doux de se reposer	RAVEL
Mildred Hunter, flute; Hermann Busch, cello	
Chantes et danses de la mort: Trépak, Berceuse,	
Sérénade, Le Chef d'armée	MOUSSORGSKY

Martial Singher was in voice yesterday afternoon. He made the Town Hall ring and vibrate. He also, at the end of his program, made this wearied intelligencer sit up and listen. For his rendering of Moussorgsky's tragic *Songs and Dances of Death* was a vocal reading (in French) of such dramatic intensity as has not been experienced by your reviewer previously this season, or often in any.

The program was a good one and the whole afternoon a delight, from the spacious eighteenth-century arias of Bach and Gluck and Rameau to Ravel's picturesque and acidulous evocations of Madagascar, sung on this occasion to their proper accompaniment of cello, piano, and flute. There were also five tasteful, if somewhat thin, songs by Reynaldo Hahn and two sturdy bits from de Falla. The latter of these, the finale from *Master Peter's Puppet Show,* even when accompanied by only a pianoforte, is a handsome number indeed. Mr. Singher's rousing rendition of it (in Spanish) made one regret that nobody ever gives us any more the full dramatic version of *El Retablo.*

The Hahn songs gave us Mr. Singher at his most charming. A concert version of the salon style is not an easy note to achieve, but Mr. Singher observed it with all the grace (and some of the unction) of a French restaurateur. If Hahn's songs are not quite first-class provender, they are none the less delicate cuisine; and no public's taste for them can be reproached. They are hot-house Parnassian poetry blended to suave melodies and set off by delicate accompaniments, bland nourishment, a little monotonous each. Sung in anything but half-tints and perfect French, they are unendurable. Impeccably presented, they become, if not works of art, a luxury product of distinction.

Moussorgsky's four vast pieces (cantatas really) called *The Songs and Dances of Death* are as real as war and very nearly as terrifying. They are hugely varied, dramatic, intense, and musically of the highest beauty. Few singers attempt them, and fewer make of them anything but a tedious proof of devotion. In Mr. Singher's hands they came to life so vividly and with such grandeur that the whole house, as well as your critic, sat enthralled, immobilized by their terror and their beauty.

For this work, as for the others, Paul Ulanowsky provided accompaniments for any singer to dream about and audiences to pray for. Mildred Hunter, flutist, and Hermann Busch, cellist, played with him not at all ungracefully in Ravel's *Chansons Madécasses*.

January 19, 1948

The Accents of Passion

ELENA NIKOLAIDI, contralto, recital last night in Town Hall. Accompanist, JAN BEHR.

ARIA, "Nel lasciarti," from *Olimpiade*	CIMAROSA
Im Abendroth; Im Freien; Romanze; Ungeduld	SCHUBERT
Mignon; Storchenbotschaft; Zigeunerin	WOLF
ARIA from *Euryanthe*	WEBER
Lieder eines fahrenden Gesellen: Wenn mein Schatz Hochzeit macht; Ging heut' Abend über's Feld; Ich hab' ein glühend Messer; Die zwei blauen Augen	MAHLER
TWO GREEK FOLKSONGS: *Neranzoula,* MARGARITIS; *Lullaby,*	PONIRIDIS
Seguidilla	DE FALLA
Coplas de Carro Dulce	OBRADORS

Elena Nikolaidi, who sang last night in the Town Hall, is Greek by birth and German trained. Her voice, an alto by its weight and dark color, is wide of range and spectacularly powerful at the top. Her personal beauty is of the Juno type, with facial expressions and bodily attitudes of the highest dramatic expressivity. She is clearly an artist, a musician, and an actress.

Last night her program, mostly German, ran from Weber and Schubert through Wolf and Mahler. The language of these composers she projected impeccably, and she sang their tunes on pitch. She added drama, too, to their communication, staged everything, so to speak, and that most impressively.

Her dramatic accents, indeed, were more impressive than appropriate. Filling the house with sound and with large, plain emotional meaning is an operatic procedure not necessarily advantageous to the intimacies of lieder. Miss Nikolaidi sounded well and looked striking while doing this, but stylistically her work was exaggerated.

Vocally it was also excessive by moments, as if she felt sheer loudness were a virtue. Loudness does give an intrinsic pleasure, of course, when the voice is rich, vibrant, and handsomely colored. But the ultimate in loudness is rarely becoming to settings of lyric poetry, and it does tire the voice. Last night the artist had used her powers vocal and dramatic with such freedom that when she came to sing Eglantine's aria from Weber's *Euryanthe*—the only piece on the program that justified such emphasis—she found herself screaming, if ever so little, on the high notes and unable to articulate clearly the rapid scales.

It is possible that Miss Nikolaidi, an extrovert Mediterranean talent, has missed as much as she has gained from her Central European schooling. I am sure she believes deeply in German lieder. But I could not help wishing last night that she would stop worrying this repertory and sing more Verdi, for which she appears to be gifted like few. The minutiae of sentiment and poesy are not for her. She belongs, I believe, to the accents of passion and to the bravura style.

October 11, 1949

Lovely Voice, Perfect Taste

Helen Thigpen, soprano, recital last night in Town Hall. Assisting pianist, Hellmut Baerwald.

Here the Deities Approve; Strike the Viol	Purcell, ed. Edmunds
Not All My Torments; Man is for Woman Made	Purcell, ed. Britten
La Mort d'Ophélie, Op. 18; *Villanelle; Le Spectre de la Rose*	Berlioz
Aria, *Non temer amato bene*	Mozart
Violin obbligato, Frank Kneisel	
Auf ein altes Bild; Lebe Wohl; Nimmersatte Liebe; Neue Liebe	Wolf
The Valley; The Negro Speaks of Rivers; Night Song; Joy	Swanson

Helen Thigpen sang last night in the Town Hall, giving great joy. The joy came from her lovely voice, from her program of rare and handsome works, and from her distinguished musicianship. Not often of a winter does one hear a vocal evening of song so high-class all round.

Three works by Berlioz and four by Howard Swanson were an

especial delight, being both unfamiliar as recital fare and in themselves *grande cuisine*. The Berlioz *Death of Ophelia* is one of the great French long songs, perhaps the model of them all. *The Ghost of a Rose* and the *Villanelle* are no less perfect, no less musically imaginative; but the Ophelia piece is longer, grander, evocative of a more spacious picture. Miss Thigpen gave them all to us with clarity and breadth.

Howard Swanson is a composer whose work singers (and pianists, too) should look into. It is refined in sentiment, sophisticated of line and harmony in a way not at all common among American music writers. His songs have a delicate elaboration of thought and an intensity of feeling that recall Fauré. Of the four sung last night only one, *The Negro Speaks of Rivers*, overstated its subject; and here the fault, I think, was largely that of the poet, Langston Hughes. The other three are a contribution to song repertory. One is grateful to Miss Thigpen for singing them, doubly for interpreting them so sensitively.

Sensitivity, as a matter of fact, is this artist's most imposing quality. That and her high standards of musical taste. She phrases; she pronounces; she floats a musical line; she keeps a rhythm; she makes beautiful sounds; she stays on pitch. All the musical amenities are hers. If occasionally she croons a bit, she is also mistress of the finest spun, the most penetrating true pianissimo now available, to my knowledge, on the American concert stage. She is an artist and a musician through and through.

Her voice, one of great natural beauty, is a lyric soprano of no extraordinary range or volume; yet it sails high with comfort and is not wanting in dramatic accents or in vibrancy. Its greatest warmth is in the lower and middle ranges. Its greatest natural appeal, however, its special quality of sweetness, lies at the top. Here it is an impersonal vibration, utterly true acoustically, a little disembodied, as resonant as an E string or a flute. Concert experience will give it, I imagine, more body. It is not a weak voice, but it does tend to dissociate itself now and then from the producing artist. At such moments it loses no beauty; the music sung merely ceases to be a human communication and becomes a sort of angelic sound-effect.

50

Miss Thigpen's whole vocal production is that of one who cares for loveliness. With more stage experience, and with her already great musical authority, she should be a recitalist of the first class.

November 17, 1949

"La Môme" Piaf

The presence among us of Edith ("la Môme") Piaf, currently singing at the Playhouse, is a reminder, and a very pleasant one, that the French *chanson* is an art form as traditional as the concert song. It has a glorious history and a vast repertory. Its dead authors and composers have streets named after them. Its living ones, just like the writers of operas, symphonies, and oratorios, enjoy a prestige that is not expressed in their income level. Its interpreters are artists in the highest sense of the term, easily distinguishable in this regard from the stars of commercialized entertainment.

If the official art music of our time expresses largely the life and ideals of the bourgeoisie and penetrates to the basic strata of society *from above*, the *chanson* is almost wholly occupied with depicting contemporary life from the viewpoint of the underprivileged and comes to us *from below*. The habitats of the official style are dressy places with a sanctimonious air about them. The *chanson* lives in neighborhood "music halls," as the French call them, or what we refer to, using a French term, as "vaudeville" houses. The *chanson* has nothing to do with farm life, either. Farm workers, unless they are itinerants who spend their winters in town, sing, when they sing at all, an older repertory, that which we denominate folklore. The *chanson* is a musical art form of the urban proletariat.

Its social origins and preoccupations are expressed not only in the words of the songs but also, in performance, by a vocal style opposed in method to that of the vocal studios. The latter consider high notes their greatest glory and make every effort, in training the voice, to spread the quality of these downward through the middle and chest ranges. The *chansonniers* use principally chest resonances, carrying these as high in the vocal range as possible and avoiding pure head tone as rigorously as singers of the official school avoid an unmixed chest tone. Head tone is used, if at all, for comic or character effects, to represent the voices of children, of the not very bright, and of the socially hoity-toity.

Miss Piaf represents the art of the *chansonnière* at its most classical. The vocalism is styled and powerful; her diction is clarity itself; her phrasing and gestures are of the simplest. Save for a slight tendency to overuse the full arm swing with index finger pointed, she has literally no personal mannerisms. She stands in the middle of a bare stage in the classic black dress of medium length, her hair tinted red and tousled, as is equally classical (Yvette Guilbert, Polaire, and Damia all wore it so), her feet planted about six inches apart; and she never moves, except for the arms. Even with these her gestures are sparing, and she uses them as much for abstractly rhetorical as for directly expressive purposes.

There is apparently not a nerve in her body. Neither is there any pretense of relaxation. She is not tense but intense, in no way spontaneous, just thoroughly concentrated and impersonal. Her power of dramatic projection is tremendous. She is a great technician because her methods are of the simplest. She is a great artist because she gives you a clear vision of the scene or subject she is depicting with a minimum injection of personality. Such a concentration at once of professional authority and of personal modesty is both delightful and no end impressive.

If Miss Piaf had not impressed me so deeply with the authenticity of her repertory and her convictions about its rendering, I should have used my column today for praising Les Compagnons de la Chanson, a male chorus of nine singers who precede her on the program. They sing folksongs to the accompaniment of athletic pantomime with a perfection of drill, vocal and muscular, that is both sidesplitting and utterly charming. If anybody wants to find a political reference in their song about a bear that terrified the village but became, when legally elected, as good a mayor as his predecessor, I presume such an interpretation could be discovered without too much effort, since otherwise the number has little point. Their imitation of an American radio quartet accompanied by a swing band, however, needs no further point than its excellent satire. Their work in every number is funny and unusually imaginative. "La Môme," or "Pal" Piaf, to translate her cognomen, may be strong meat, artistically speaking, for American theater audiences, though I hope our public will long go on loving and applauding her. But Les Compagnons are more the sort of act we can take without effort. I must say they are easy to enjoy.

November 9, 1947

Personal Distinction

MARGARET TRUMAN, soprano, in American Broadcasting Company's "Carnegie Hall" program last night, with ROBERT SHAW CHORUS, and Orchestra, DR. FRANK BLACK conducting.

WALTZ from *The Sleeping Beauty* — TCHAIKOVSKY
Dr. Frank Black and Orchestra

"O mio Babbino Caro," from *Gianni Schicchi* — PUCCINI
Margaret Truman and Orchestra

OVERTURE to *Hänsel und Gretel* — HUMPERDINCK
Dr. Frank Black and Orchestra

Christmas Echo Song — HUGO JUNGST
Robert Shaw Chorus

Carol of the Bells — LEONTOWITCH
Robert Shaw Chorus

Dance of the Chinese Dolls from *The Christmas Tree Suite* — REBIKOFF
Dr. Frank Black and Orchestra

O, Little Town of Bethlehem — REDNER
Margaret Truman and Robert Shaw Chorus

Adeste Fideles   TRADITIONAL
                        Robert Shaw Chorus
Silent Night   GRUBER
              Margaret Truman and Robert Shaw Chorus

Margaret Truman made her first appearance as a concert artist in
New York at a short broadcast of semipopular music that took place
last night before an invited public in Carnegie Hall. She sang one
brief·aria from Puccini's *Gianni Schicchi* and two familiar Christmas carols. The rest of the program was of negligible interest to a
reviewer.

Miss Truman herself presents surely a greater personal than musical distinction. One was prepared for the grace, warmth, and refinement of her presence; but this reporter, having seen only the
grinning photographs that present-day publicity sanctions, was not
at all prepared for the beauty of her face in repose. Few artists now
appearing before the public have Miss Truman's physical advantages, and almost none other has her dignity.

Her vocal advantages are far less impressive. The voice is small
in size and range and not at all beautiful. The lower notes of it
do not project, and the upper ones are hollow. Nowhere is there any
vibrancy or richness. She seems to sing carefully, is obliged to, indeed, by the poverty of her resources. Her English enunciation in
one of the carols was remarkably clear. Of temperament, of the
quality that enables a musician to bring music to life, she seems to
have none at all. Her singing did not communicate last night as
powerfully as her personality did. Only at the end of each piece,
when she stopped singing and smiled and became the lovely Miss
Truman again, did she make real contact with the guests of the
evening.

December 21, 1949

III. OPERAS

Perfect and Powerful

SALOME, music drama in one act; libretto by OSCAR WILDE, translated into German by HEDWIG LACHMANN; music by RICHARD STRAUSS; revival last night at the Metropolitan Opera House. The cast:

Herod Antipas	*Max Lorenz*
Herodias	*Kerstin Thorborg*
Salome	*Ljuba Welitsch* (debut)
Jokanaan	*Joel Berglund*
Narraboth	*Brian Sullivan*
The Page of Herodias	*Herta Glaz*
First Nazarene	*Dezso Ernster*

Second Nazarene	*Emery Darcy*
First Jew	*Leslie Chabay*
Second Jew	*Thomas Hayward*
Third Jew	*Alessio De Paolis*
Fourth Jew	*Paul Franke*
Fifth Jew	*Gerhard Pechner*
First Soldier	*Jerome Hines*
Second Soldier	*Philip Kinsman*
A Cappadocian	*Osie Hawkins*
A Slave	*Inge Manski*

Conductor, FRITZ REINER (debut); stage director, HERBERT GRAF.

Strauss's *Salome,* restudied, refurbished, and rehearsed, was the vehicle for two debuts last night at the Metropolitan Opera House— that of Fritz Reiner, who conducted, and that of Ljuba Welitsch, who sang the name part. The occasion was instrumentally perfect, vocally well-nigh so, and dramatically sensational. Never before in the hearing of this listener has the work been led so suavely, so powerfully, or with so luxurious a sound. Rarely has it been sung so well. And only in the memory of those older opera goers who remember Fremstad, Garden, or Vix, has it ever been acted so thoroughly.

A blueprint for acting is clear in the score; but not often have we had offered us the full realization, in all its fascinating horror, of that perverse and sensual story. Miss Welitsch could not have given it to us last night without the understanding aid of Mr. Reiner, and he would have been impotent to communicate the work's full expressive sense without the detailed and courageous collaboration of a major singing actress. The whole staggering effect, moreover, had to be made possible by a solid supporting cast, clear stage direction, and plenty of rehearsal both with and without the orchestra. Under such circumstances and with such artists, the Metropolitan can produce today, did last night produce one of the great musico-dramatic performances of our century.

The score itself, like the play on which it is built, makes its effect by accumulation. When played for momentum and trajectory, without haste and without respite, it leaves one shaken. It does this by the expressive power of its orchestral textures and the elaborate organization of its expressive devices, rather than by any especial beauty or aptness in its melodic material. It is like a modernistic sculpture made of cheap wood, glass, rocks, cinders, papier-mâché, sandpaper, and bits of old fur. The material elements of it are without nobility; but the whole makes a composition, and the composition speaks. Even poorly led, sung, or acted, it speaks. Led, sung, and acted with detailed and cumulative emphasis, it is staggering both musically and emotionally.

The cast which helped Miss Welitsch and Mr. Reiner to such an effect last night was notable in the supporting roles. Max Lorenz, as Herod; Brian Sullivan, as the Young Captain; Dezso Ernster, as the First Nazarene; even Kerstin Thorborg, whose Herodias was less than striking vocally; and, above all, Joel Berglund, whose Prophet was in every way handsome—all were part of a team and a first-class team. Everybody on the stage, down to the last slave and soldier, was playing in a play; and they were all playing in the same play, just as the musicians in the pit were all playing the same piece. The result, at that level of talent and skill and with a script of that strength, was overpowering, though nobody screamed or blasted.

Detailed examination of the leading soprano's vocal qualities must await further appearances. So must any recounting of the excellent *Gianni Schicchi* performance, full of fine Italian singing and stage work, which started off the evening. It will certainly be a pleasure, too, to follow Fritz Reiner's work in the theater, long a delight in the concert hall and now fully revealed as great opera conducting, the greatest, I should think, that we have heard here in several decades.

February 5, 1949

Musically Authentic

PELLÉAS ET MÉLISANDE, opera in five acts; libretto by MAURICE MAETERLINCK; music by CLAUDE DEBUSSY; first production by the New York City Opera Company last night at the New York City Center. The cast:

Mélisande	*Maggie Teyte* (debut)
Geneviève	*Mary Kreste*
Yniold	*Virginia Haskins*
Pelléas	*Fernand Martel* (debut)
Golaud	*Carlton Gauld*
Arkel	*Norman Scott*
Physician	*Arthur Newman*

Conductor, JEAN MOREL; designer and stage director, THEODORE KOMISARJEVSKY.

Debussy's *Pelléas et Mélisande,* as produced last night by the New York City Opera Company at the City Center of Music and Drama, marked another advance in the achievements of both institutions. Musically it was a delight, and verbally it was clear. If the visual aspect of the performance was in general unsatisfactory, that was a not ineradicable blot on a distinguished piece of work.

Credit for that distinction goes first to Jean Morel, who conducted a reading at once beautiful and authentic. His cast, headed by Maggie Teyte, did beautiful work musically. Their movements may be more convincing at later performances. At present these are tentative, because a unit set of unbelievable ugliness and ineptitude keeps everybody climbing up and down stairs and over curbstones. Full freedom of action on such a cluttered stage is not to be expected ever.

Miss Teyte sang beautifully. So did Mary Kreste, as Geneviève. Carlton Gauld, as Golaud, was the best of all, though the role lies a shade high for him. Virginia Haskins, as Yniold, was excellent. Norman Scott, as Arkel, was a pleasure, too. Fernand Martel, a Canadian, who sang Pelléas, got better as the evening went on. He is not yet at home, I think, on stages and does not project completely. His voice, though pretty, is neither large nor expressive;

and he mouths a bit, singing the while in his throat. But he has musical taste and sings a lovely French.

Everybody, in fact, sang good French, pronounced it clearly, made that, rather than mere vocalization, the object of the evening. Consequently the singing all had color in it and variety. Diction, expressivity of timbre, and a care for the musical amenities made of the whole performance a pleasure. And it was not, surprisingly enough, very much more Miss Teyte's show than anybody else's, though, of course, her experience with the whole repertory of Debussy's vocal works did give her an edge on the others for interpretation.

Miss Teyte was grand, if also a bit stiff. But the real hero of the occasion was Jean Morel. If we heard more French works prepared with his care and his understanding, we might all go oftener to the opera. Because French opera is the one repertory that makes today dramatic as well as musical sense. Unfortunately it was only the musical (and the verbal) sense that came over last night. I recommend listening to this show with the eyes closed.

March 26, 1948

In Fairy Tale Vein

DAS RHEINGOLD, text and music by RICHARD WAGNER; first performance in the afternoon subscription series of *Der Ring des Nibelungen*, sponsored by the Metropolitan Opera Guild, yesterday at the Metropolitan Opera House. The cast:

Wotan	*Joel Berglund*
Donner	*Kenneth Schon*
Froh	*Emery Darcy*
Loge	*Max Lorenz*
Alberich	*Gerhard Pechner*
Mime	*John Garris*

Operas 59

Fasolt	Jerome Hines
Fafner	Mihaly Szekely
Fricka	Kerstin Thorborg
Freia	Polyna Stoska
Erda	Blanche Thebom
Woglinde	Inge Manski
Wellgunde	Martha Lipton
Flosshilde	Margaret Harshaw

Conductor, FRITZ STIEDRY. Production staged by HERBERT GRAF, designed and lighted by LEE SIMONSON.

The cast, as you can verify above, was a distinguished one at yesterday afternoon's performance of *Das Rheingold*. The musical audition, too, was far more polished than most of those one hears these days at the Metropolitan Opera House. And the new scenery proved to be in every way worthy of the grandiose style that Wagner's *Ring of the Nibelungs* tetralogy demands. Particularly satisfactory was the shipshapeness with which lighting, stage movements, and scene changes were operated. It assured us that the Met can still put on a show in professional style, even when the scenic set-up is complex, and that any other kind of presentation at that establishment is attributable either to carelessness or to an attempt to make outworn material do.

Lee Simonson's sets follow in spirit and general plan the Kautsky designs with which we have long been familiar and which once bore the blessing of Bayreuth itself. Their chief departure from these is a translation of Romantic detail into modernistic detail. Mr. Simonson's rocks are more simplified, more angular than what a nineteenth-century artist would have conceived; and his Valhalla bears such a clear resemblance to the Cornell Medical Center (amplified to Radio City proportions) that it suggests some massive real estate development entitled, perhaps, "The Valhalla Apartments."

This last detail is not entirely happy, and the cubistic rocks are a bit brutal in outline. Also, the latter budge when clutched. One hopes they are better built than their present instability suggests. But everything else is tasteful and solid. Even the Worm is impressive. Particularly delightful are the giants and the dwarves. The former, shod on stilts and clothed in fur, are hugely effective; and the latter

60

are terrifyingly true to fairy-tale life. The child of any age who did not respond to both these creations would be poor indeed of spirit. The Rhine maidens appear about as usual, since their visible shape is largely determined by that of the chairs concealed beneath their trailing petticoats. They swim about, as formerly, by means of a modified breast stroke.

In an afternoon full of good singing, Jerome Hines, as Fasolt, was notable for excellence. Joel Berglund sang a euphonious Wotan, too; and Polyna Stoska, as Freia, the only soprano in the cast, emitted fine bright sounds to lighten a dark ensemble. Max Lorenz, as Loge, was a vocal relief, too, from all the basses and baritones that filled the stage; and his dramatic animation was equally grateful in those scenes, all too numerous, when there is nothing for anybody else to do but stand still. Less charming was the traditional tremolo with which Gerhard Pechner sang Alberich; and Blanche Thebom, as Erda, sang consistently a little flat.

The afternoon was otherwise agreeable for sound singing and for orchestral amenities observed. The weakest musically of all the *Ring* operas, *Das Rheingold* was all the same a pleasure for careful execution. And the new sets were not the least among the many elements responsible for the creation of a fairy-tale atmosphere in which everything took place according to mythology, both Germanically and theatrically speaking.

January 8, 1948

Specialty of the House

GÖTTERDÄMMERUNG, music drama by RICHARD WAGNER; third performance of the season at the Metropolitan Opera House Wednesday night. The cast:

Siegfried	*Set Svanholm*
Gunther	*Osie Hawkins*
Hagen	*Dezso Ernster*
Alberich	*Gerhard Pechner*
Brünnhilde	*Helen Traubel*
Gutrune	*Polyna Stoska*
Waltraute	*Kerstin Thorborg*
Woglinde	*Inge Manski*
Wellgunde	*Lucielle Browning*
Flosshilde	*Herta Glaz*
First Norn	*Jean Browning-Madeira*
Second Norn	*Lucielle Browning*
Third Norn	*Jeanne Palmer*
Two Vassals	{*Emery Darcy* / *Philip Kinsman*}

Conductor, FRITZ STIEDRY. Production staged by HERBERT GRAF, designed and lighted by LEE SIMONSON.

Richard Wagner's *Twilight of the Gods*, as performed on Wednesday night at the Metropolitan Opera House, lasted from half-past seven till five minutes of twelve (a saving of five minutes on the normal run); and there was not, for this listener, a dull moment in the second half. The first act and a half were talky, save for two fine orchestral interludes. Dramatically and musically the script just will not move along. But beginning about the middle of the second act, with the entrance of the male chorus, the stage takes on animation, ensemble singing adds brilliance to the musical effect, and the whole work grows in grandeur until the final curtain falls. A wealth of musical thought and an opulent elaboration of musical textures pile up for two hours, till it is impossible, given a reasonably good musical rendering, to leave the theater without some feeling of fullness, of fulfillment.

Wednesday's rendering was, moreover, far better than reasonably good. It was first-class clean through, thoroughly grand and wonderful. The orchestral direction of Fritz Stiedry, the singing of Helen Traubel, Set Svanholm, and Dezso Ernster, were what anybody could know for memorable. Refinement, power, and beauty marked the reading in all its leading roles; dignity and musicianship in the secondary ones gave shape to the whole. Even the stage movement, deliberately static and statuesque, was executed with decorum. And the scenery, new last year, is still, along with the costumes that go with it, an integrated, harmonious design and reasonably clean.

It becomes increasingly evident to this observer that Wagner's works are the branch of repertory for which the Met, in the present decade, is best adapted. The German-language singers available there are far superior to those whose preparation has destined them chiefly for Italian, French, or English-language work. So are the present staff conductors of German training. And eminently suitable is the size of the house and stage. Wagner fills the place with resonance and visibility. Big sounds, big scenic effects, fires, mountains, vast sunsets, demolitions, and characters whose emotions and conflicts are as huge and as impersonal as those of any leviathan—all are at home in that house and becoming to it.

Set Svanholm's slender figure is of no help to Wagner, though his handsome singing is. Wagner's music dramas are conceived for a theater of whales. These move slowly, relentlessly, on an epic scale, require space, offer sounds of infinite power and complexity to fill up that space. At the Met, they and the house are of a proportion. Italian opera has never since Caruso's death been loud enough for it, and French opera never has been loud like that at any time.

The management and executants, moreover, seem to take Wagner for music's central figure. They work more carefully for him, more confidently, and with more dignity, project a sense of having studied everything more thoroughly than is apparent in the rest of the repertory. Occasionally another composer gets a fair deal; but Wagner always gets the best of everything—the best playing, the best singing, the best scenery, the best direction and lighting, the most impressive effects of every kind. It is as if only he were worthy the deployment of so vast a machine. The contrast between these works and the rest of opera, as given year after year in that house, is striking and revelatory. Not of Wagner's musical primacy, however. Mozart and Bizet remain greater composers and more expert men of the theater, and Verdi is at least his equal. But it does show us what the Met, its whole set-up and management, are good for. Good *for* because good *at*.

January 21, 1949

Louise as a Wan Blonde

LOUISE, musical romance in four acts; music by GUSTAVE CHARPEN-TIER; revival at the Metropolitan Opera House last night. The cast:

Louise	*Dorothy Kirsten*
Julien	*Raoul Jobin*
The Mother	*Margaret Harshaw*
The Father	*John Brownlee*
Irma	*Maxine Stellman*
Camille; Artichoke Vendor	*Thelma Votipka*
Gertrude	*Herta Glaz*
The Apprentice; Street Arab	*Lillian Raymondi*
Elise; Milk Woman	*Inge Manski*
Blanche	*Irene Jordan*
Suzanne; Young Ragpicker	*Martha Lipton*
The Forewoman	*May Savage*
Marguerite; Newspaper Girl; Bird Food Vendor	*Paula Lenchner*
The Painter; Rag Vendor	*George Cehanovsky*
First Philosopher	*Lorenzo Alvary*
Second Philosopher	*Osie Hawkins*
The Sculptor	*Clifford Harvuot*
The Poet	*John Garris*
The Student; Carrot Vendor	*Lodovico Oliviero*
Song Writer	*Hugh Thompson*
Noctambulist	*Thomas Hayward*
King of the Fools	*Alessio De Paolis*
First Policeman; Green Peas Vendor	*Emery Darcy*

64

Second Policeman	*Lawrence Davidson*
Coal Picker; Watercress Vendor	*Thelma Altman*
Ragpicker	*Nicola Moscona*
Junk Man	*Philip Kinsman*
Old Clothes Man	*Leslie Chabay*
Street Sweeper; Chair Mender Madeleine;	*Evelyn Sachs* (debut)

Conductor, Louis Fourestier; stage director, Désiré Defrère; chorus master, Kurt Adler. Ballet soloist, Marina Svetlova; choreography by Boris Romanoff.

Charpentier's *Louise,* which was heard again last night at the Metropolitan Opera House after nearly a five-year interval, is a good play and a good score. The play, incidentally, is not by Charpentier, as the printed program states and as the printed score would lead one to believe, but by the poet Saint-Pol-Roux and is so registered at the Société des Auteurs Dramatiques, in the rue Ballu. The present Metropolitan production of this sound and charming work is still visually evocative of the turn of this century and auditively agreeable in the small roles. It lacks force and brilliance at the key positions, all of them, including that of the conductor. Consequently the show is pale and cold.

Dorothy Kirsten, in the title role, would seem deliberately to have affected pallor. She wears the palest of yellow hair, the wishy-washiest of pinks in her dresses, and an almost dead-white make-up. Her voice seems light for the role, too; and though she sings most prettily and pronounces clearly, she does not come over vocally as a character of much emotional weight. Even her acting is puny. She represents Louise as constantly clutching at things and people, constantly weeping and constantly pitying herself. The absence of physical alacrity from Miss Kirsten's movements, the insistence on an extreme and obviously artifical blondness (if she expects to pass for a Paris working girl) in her get-up, and an almost crooned song-speech end by giving to her whole interpretation a suggestion of Mae West. She has worked hard and prepared her reading carefully, but I think she has missed the point of Louise.

The latter is no tender bourgeoise wrapped up in pink silk shirtwaists all for love. She is a working girl brought up on socialism, adding thus to the normal revolt of youth a certain political and philosophic education. She would leave home shortly in any case. Her mother knows this only too well and hopes to keep her under guard till an offer of legitimate marriage in her own class turns up. Louise, however, is more interested in emancipation than in working; and when Julien offers her, along with socialist conversation and the independence of the artist's life, the full doctrine and practice of free love, it is perfectly clear that the family is not going to see much more of her. Even if Julien should not pan out, her decision is made. Home and mother have lost.

Here I am telling what the opera *Louise* ought to be like instead of what it was like last night. It was a clean performance but a lifeless one, save for the small roles. One of these was charmingly sung by a newcomer to the house, Evelyn Sachs. The most disappointing of the principals were Miss Kirsten, Mr. Brownlee, and the conductor Mr. Fourestier. Mr. Jobin and Miss Harshaw were not always convincing dramatically, but at least they made some noise. The performance was lifeless at the top.

December 13, 1947

Toscanini's *Aïda*

AÏDA, opera with music by GIUSEPPE VERDI; text by ANTONIO GHISLANZONI; Acts I and II, broadcast from Studio 8-H, Radio City yesterday evening with ARTURO TOSCANINI conducting the N.B.C. Symphony Orchestra. The cast:

Aïda	*Herva Nelli*
Amneris	*Eva Gustavson*
Priestess	*Teresa Stitch Randall*
Radames	*Richard Tucker*
Amonasro	*Giuseppe Valdengo*

66

Ramfis	Norman Scott
King of Egypt	Dennis Harbour
Messenger	Virginio Assandri

Chorus of sixty voices directed by ROBERT SHAW

Once a year Arturo Toscanini, who conducts operas better than almost anybody else but who will not work with the Metropolitan, gives us the music of one by means of radio. Yesterday afternoon the first half of Verdi's *Aïda* was our fare, and next week the other half will be coming along. The N.B.C. Symphony Orchestra provides the instrumental support. Singers are listed above. The real star, of course, is the Maestro himself, showing us by means of music alone what dramatic animation means and how it need not at any point make war on clarity.

The Maestro, broadcasting, takes advantage of the fact that no distracting visual element or stage necessity is present to act as a brake. His music flows like running water, hasting o'er pebble and sand; and the sound of it is every bit as refreshing. His opera performances are limpid, lucid, expeditious. You hear the whole texture of the score better than you ever could in an opera house or from the broadcast of a full theatrical execution. They are a privilege, a pleasure, and, for all their distortion through speed, a model of pacing.

The faults of yesterday's *Aïda* lay on the vocal side. The singers were not poor singers, but neither was any one of them quite up to the occasion. They kept up with the Maestro's pace all right and mostly sang on (or near) the pitch. They had pleasant voices. They mostly wabbled a little, and they did not seem to have invariably a sure placement. What effect they gave in the hall I cannot imagine, since I could get no hint from the broadcast about the real volume of any of them. It sounded to me as if the soloists were too close to the microphone and the choral singers too far away.

Some engineering fault, moreover, either at the studio or in my machine (which is supposed to be a good one) made the voices seem to spread and blare and buzz. The Priestess, for instance, as sung by Teresa Stitch Randall, might easily have been two Teresa Stitch Randalls singing together. A double auditory image was present whenever she sang, also a huge and barnlike reverberation. This effect was engineering trickery, I am sure, because it came on and off with the temple music. It was not entirely pleasant to the ear or resembling, for Mrs. Randall's voice is in real life remarkable for its clarity of focus.

Engineering also played tricks on the scene between Amneris and Aïda by varying the volume in such a way (or possibly by not correctly adjusting it) that they seemed to be yards apart, though their conversation at this point is intimate. Who was responsible (engineers or artists) for the lack of vocal glamour in the two big arias, the tenor and soprano ones, I should not care to guess. Nor why the choral ensembles, all of them, lacked penetration in the soprano element. Perhaps it is thought not important, when the Maestro conducts, what the voices sound like. It is his show, not theirs. Well, his instruments sounded well yesterday and balanced brightly. I suspect that a change of acoustical set-up is needed for his opera broadcasts, if their vocal effects are to be a match for their instrumental perfection and for the brilliance of the Maestro's rocketlike readings.

March 27, 1949

Give the Singers a Break

Every time a reviewer describes a musical performance that happens also to have been broadcast, differing evidence comes to him from listeners who were not present. In the hall, opinions differ widely about the artistic value of a musical action; but those accustomed to musical audition are not likely to be far apart in their estimate of just and unjust musical balances and of whether a given singer sang predominantly on pitch. It is like tasting lemonade; almost anybody can identify the mixture correctly as sweet or sour. One's preference in either direction remains a personal factor, a legitimate one, of course, but merely personal. Transmission by radio gives a different musical mixture from the original one and brings forth, in consequence, differing testimony. Radio listeners do not vary among themselves about the facts any more than those present at the performance do; but what they hear has small relation, as acoustical balance, to what was heard in the house. Microphone placement and the dial adjustments of the engineer in charge can either destroy an equilibrium or, in some cases, produce one.

Strauss's *Der Rosenkavalier,* as heard at the Metropolitan Opera House on the opening night of the season and as heard in some five or six American cities by television broadcast, would seem, if one pools the evidence, to have been two different performances. Only when one separates those present from those not present does the testimony make sense. In the house the singers were hard to hear, especially during the first act. There is pretty general agreement about that. The television broadcast, whether heard here or in Detroit, seems to have caused no such discomfort. The only witness who has told me otherwise turns out to have been listening in a saloon, where distractions may have made concentration incomplete. The second act, in the opera house, brought better stage-and-pit cooperation but was still, to this listener, a bit loud from the pit. The third act he did not hear.

This sifting of evidence is merely preliminary to a further discussion of the work and its performance. I must insist that whatever I say about the Metropolitan opera performances is based on what I hear at the Metropolitan Opera House. The broadcasts are another story. And what I heard on opening night seems to have been just about what everybody else heard who was present. The overbalance of sonorities in the orchestra's favor was, moreover, the work of the great Fritz Reiner—an impeccable ear, an impeccable musician, and a specialist of Richard Strauss. I am not presuming, therefore, any accident or inefficiency. I take it that a performance so handsomely cast and so thoroughly rehearsed could only have been the one he wished us to hear. And it is with full respect for so experienced an operatic director and in full awareness of the hazard that my own opinion of the work may be an isolated one, that I venture to differ with Mr. Reiner's conception.

Some fifteen years ago I heard this conductor give the same work at the Academy of Music in Philadelphia. The soloists were of top quality; the Philadelphia Orchestra was in the pit; rehearsals had been plentiful. The musical effect was much the same as that heard recently at the Metropolitan. It was that of an orchestral piece with vocal accompaniment. Now here is where I presume to differ with Mr. Reiner. I do not find such a conception of *Der Rosenkavalier* either theatrically effective or musically satisfactory. Such an approach to Wagner's *Götterdämmerung* is far more convincing, though there is some question about its being the composer's own. It works beautifully with Strauss's *Salome,* as we heard it last year under this same conductor. But *Götterdämmerung* and *Salome* are slow-moving tragic stories; emotional expansion is appropriate to them, gives them power. *Der Rosenkavalier,* a comedy of sentiment, needs lightness of hand, a mercurial wit, and all the charm possible on the stage.

It does not seem proper to me that the singing actors in this work should be treated like bellowing statues. I think they should be given their ease, encouraged to pronounce, and allowed to both sing their lines and play the play. Such a treatment need require no violation of Strauss's score. It would merely mean asking the orchestra for transparent sounds. Mr. Reiner, fully aware the other evening that certain of his singers were not being heard, held the accompaniment for pages on end to a low dynamic level. But he never got the opacity out of it. A single clarinet, using the round tone, was sufficient to eat up Eleanor Steber's voice. Now Miss Steber's voice is a beautiful one and not weak, but its projection was subject to orchestral interference. I believe that interference to have been largely an acoustical effect due to the use of excessive instrumental vibrato and similar devices for achieving a rich tonal color. I know, further, that a rich tonal color in the orchestra, especially when the scoring is elaborate, is very hard to sing against. Only the most powerful voices can compete with it. And throwing this particular opera, or any other comedy, indeed, into a key of vocal strain removes a great deal of its playing quality as drama and almost all its possibilities for vocal charm.

The above observations apply equally to Verdi's *Falstaff* and to Wagner's *Die Meistersinger*. All three of these operatic comedies, over and above their complex orchestral commentary, need clarity of stage speech and ease of stage movement. Neither can be obtained from singers who are preoccupied constantly with giving their sonorous all. I am convinced that these works would make their dramatic points better and lose no musical interest if the musicians who conduct them would let the dramatic line dominate. The musical line, in that case, would suffer, I am sure, no injury; and the musico-dramatic spectacle would be stronger. Such a change in Metropolitan habits would require, of course, a good deal more stage rehearsal than is customary or convenient; but the result, if tastefully operated, might well delight both the music-minded and the play-minded. Certainly it would put the singers into a more graceful position than the one they now occupy, in which only the microphone public can hear what they are doing.

December 4, 1949

Success Tactics

PETER GRIMES, opera in three acts and a prologue; libretto by MONTAGU SLATER derived from the poem of GEORGE CRABBE; music by BENJAMIN BRITTEN. First New York performance last night at the Metropolitan Opera House. The cast:

December 4, 1949

Peter Grimes	*Frederick Jagel*
Ellen Orford	*Regina Resnik*
Captain Balstrode	*John Brownlee*
Auntie	*Claramae Turner*

Operas 71

Two Nieces	*Paula Lenchner, Maxine Stellman*
Bob Boles	*Thomas Hayward*
Swallow	*Jerome Hines*
Mrs. (Nabob) Sedley	*Martha Lipton*
Rev. Horace Adams	*John Garris*
Ned Keene	*Hugh Thompson*
A Lawyer	*Lodovico Oliviero*
Hobson	*Philip Kinsman*
A Fisherwoman	*Thelma Altman*
A Fisherman	*Lawrence Davidson*
Dr. Thorpe	*Orrin Hill*
Boy (John)	*P. J. Smithers*

Conductor, EMIL COOPER; stage director, DINO YANNOPOULOS; chorus master, KURT ADLER. Scenery designed and painted by JOSEPH NOVAK; costumes designed by MARY PERCY SCHENCK and executed by ANTOINE OBERDING.

Benjamin Britten's *Peter Grimes,* which was added last night to the repertory of our Metropolitan Opera, is a success. It always is. Given in any language in a house of no matter what size, it always holds the attention of an audience. As given last night "the works," so to speak, which is to say, the full mechanism, musical and scenic, of a mammoth production establishment, it still held the attention.

This is not to minimize the excellences of the present production, which are many, or the care that has gone into it, which is considerable. It is merely to point out that the steam-roller processing that our beloved Met, geared to Wagner, puts any new work through is one of the severest known tests for the strength of theatrical materials. If Mr. Britten's work came out scarcely in English, vocally loud from beginning to end, and decorated in a manner both ugly and hopelessly anachronistic, it also came through the ordeal with its music still alive and its human drama still touching.

Make no mistake about *Peter Grimes.* It is varied, interesting, and solidly put together. It works. It is not a piece of any unusual flavor or distinction. It adds nothing to the history of the stage or to the history of music. But it is a rattling good repertory melodrama. And if the executant artists, beginning with Emil Cooper, who conducted, going on through Frederick Jagel and Regina Resnik, who sang the tenor and soprano leads, to the smallest role in a large cast and even including the chorus, treated the work with no consideration

72

for its special or poetic subject matter, but rather as disembodied, or "pure," theater, just "wow" material, that is exactly what the composer himself has done, what his score invites and asks for.

There is everything in it to make an opera pleasing and effective. There is a trial scene, a boat, a church (with organ music), a pub (with drinking song for the full ensemble), a storm, a night club seen through a window (with boogie-woogie music off stage and shadow play), a scene of flagellation, a mad scene, and a death. There are set-pieces galore, all different, all musically imaginative, and mostly fun. And there are a good half-dozen intermezzos, most of which are musically pretty weak but expressive all the same.

The musical structure of the opera is simple and efficient. Everything and everybody has a motif, a tune or turn of phrase that identifies. The entire orchestral structure, and most of the vocal, is pieced together out of these in the manner of Italian *verismo*. The harmony is a series of pedal-points broadly laid out to hold together the bits-and-pieces motif continuity. There is no pretense of musical development through these motifs, as in Wagner. They are pure identification tags, as in Dwight Fiske. The music is wholly objective and calculated for easy effect. That is why it works.

It works even in spite of its none too happy handling of English vowel quantities. It sacrifices these systematically, in fact, to characteristic melodic turns, as if the composer had counted from the beginning on translation. A good part of the obscurity that was characteristic of last night's diction, in spite of the singers' visible efforts to project sung speech, was due to the deliberate falsity of the prosodic line. Mr. Britten is apparently no more bothered about such niceties than he is by the anachronisms of an almost popishly High Church service in an English fishing village of 1830 and an American jazz band in the same time and place. He has gone out for theatrical effects, got them, got his success. So did the Metropolitan. And still *Peter Grimes* is not a bore.

February 13, 1948

Lively Revival

THE CRADLE WILL ROCK, opera with music and text by MARC BLITZSTEIN, performed last night at the New York City Center by the New York City Symphony, LEONARD BERNSTEIN conducting, and the following cast:

Mr. Mister	*Will Geer*
Mrs. Mister	*Shirley Booth*
Larry Foreman	*Howard da Silva*
Ella Hammer	*Muriel Smith*
Clerk	*Leonard Bernstein*
Moll	*Estelle Loring*
Gent	*Edward Brice*
Dick	*Robert Penn*
Cop	*Taggard Casey*
Rev. Salvation	*Robert Chisholm*
Editor Daily	*Brooks Dunbar*
Yasha	*Jack Albertson*
Dauber	*Chandler Cowles*
President Prexy	*Howard Blaine*
Professor Trixie	*Remo Lota*
Professor Mamie	*Edmund Hewitt*
Doctor Specialist	*Robert Pierson*
Attendant's Voice	*Hazel Shermet*
Reporter One	*Rex Coston*
Reporter Two	*Gil Houston*
Druggist	*David Thomas*
Junior Mister	*Leslie Litomy*
Sister Mister	*Jo Hurt*
Steve	*Stephen Downer*
Sadie Polock	*Marie Leidal*
Gus Polock	*Walter Scheff*
Bugs	*Edward Bryce*

Chorus of eleven singers

Marc Blitzstein's *The Cradle Will Rock,* which was performed last night at the City Center under Leonard Bernstein's direction, remains, ten years after its first New York success, one of the most charming creations of the American musical theater. It has sweetness, a cutting wit, inexhaustible fancy, and faith. One would have

74

to be untouchable (and who is?) by the aspirations of union labor to resist it. Last night's audience did not. No audience I have ever seen, in fact, and I have heard the work many times, ever has.

It was inevitable that the piece (call it, if you will, an opera, a musical comedy, or a play with music) should be revived; and it is a sound idea on Mr. Bernstein's part to revive it just now. In a year when the Left in general, and the labor movement in particular, is under attack, it is important that the Left should put its best foot forward. There is no question, moreover, but that the Left's best foot is its Left foot. In the opinion of this reviewer, Mr. Blitzstein's *Cradle* is the gayest and the most absorbing piece of musical theater that America's Left has inspired. Long may it prosper, long may it remind us that union cards are as touchy a point of honor as marriage certificates.

The Cradle is a fairy tale, with villains and a hero. Like all fairy tales, it is perfectly true. It is true because it makes you believe it. If the standard Broadway "musical" plugs what Thurman Arnold called "the folklore of capitalism," this play with (or "in") music recites with passion and piety the mythology of the labor movement. It is not a reflective or a realistic work. There is not one original thought or actual observation in it. Everybody is a type, symbolizes something; and the whole is a morality play. Its power is due in large part to the freshness, in terms of current entertainment repertory, of the morality that it expounds. That morality is a prophetic and confident faith in trade unionism as a dignifying force morally, as well as economically.

An equally large part of its power comes from its author's talent for musical caricature. He makes fun of his characters from beginning to end by musical means. Sometimes his fun is tender, as in the love duet of the Polish couple; and sometimes it is mean, as in the songs of Junior and Sister Mister. But always there is a particular musical style to characterize each person or scene; and always that style is aptly chosen, pungently taken off. The work has literary imperfections but musically not one fault of style.

Its presentation last night followed the style of its 1937 production, save for the substitution of Mr. Bernstein at a small orchestra in place of Mr. Blitzstein at a small piano. As before, there were costumes but no props or scenery. As before, the system of presentation was completely effective, though the orchestra added little musically. The cast was fair, some of it excellent, notably Will Geer and Howard da Silva, who had sung Mr. Mister and Larry Foreman in the original performances. Muriel Smith, as Ella Hammer, sang her scene charmingly; Shirley Booth, as Mrs. Mister, got constant laughs; and Estelle Loring, as the Moll, did a professional job. The others were less than ideal, but that made little difference. The work is a tough one and hard to spoil. It was not spoiled. It was played with love and received a rousing welcome home.

November 25, 1947

Little Musical Foxes

REGINA, musical drama based on Lillian Hellman's *The Little Foxes;* libretto and music by MARC BLITZSTEIN; first performance last night in the Forty-sixth Street Theater. The cast:

Addie	*Lillyn Brown*
Cal	*William Warfield*
Alexandra Biddens	*Priscilla Gillette*
Chinkypin	*Philip Hepburn*
Jazz	*William Dillard*
Angel Band	*Bernard Addison, Buster Bailey, Rudy Nichols, Benny Morton*
Regina Giddens	*Jane Pickens*
Birdie Hubbard	*Brenda Lewis*
Oscar Hubbard	*David Thomas*
Leo Hubbard	*Russell Nype*
Marshall	*Donald Clarke*
Ben Hubbard	*George Lipton*
Belle	*Clarisse Crawford*

76

Pianist	*Marion Carley*
Violinist	*Alfred Bruning*
Horace Giddens	*William Wilderman*
Manders	*Lee Sweetland*
Ethelinda	*Peggy Turnley*

Conductor, MAURICE ABRAVANEL; stage director, ROBERT LEWIS. Dances by ANNA SOKOLOW; settings designed by HORACE ARMISTEAD; costumes by ALINE BERNSTEIN.

Whether Marc Blitzstein's *Regina* is an improvement on Lillian Hellman's original play is not for this reviewer to judge. His only concern is with its intrinsic quality as musical theater; and that is none too easy to perceive through the presentation at the Forty-sixth Street Theater. The latter, unfortunately for the music-eared, is not very musical, though it is unqestionably very, very, very, very theater. The play, the spectacle, has certainly a high degree of sustained dramatic tension; it is no bore. There are also moments of musical delight. But by and large the tonal habiliment of the script, as performed, is raucous in sound, coarse in texture, explosive, obstreperous, and strident.

Exceptions to the generally unmusical quality of the rendering are the excellent voices of Brenda Lewis and Priscilla Gillette. William Wilderman, too, is vocally adequate. And Jane Pickens has a clarity of singing speech that is in every way admirable. The rest of the cast is without musical distinction. Even the orchestra, directed by no less a musician than Maurice Abravanel, has a splintery sound. It doesn't blend, and it doesn't support. It either drowns the singers or disappears.

The musical composition is that of an incomplete opera, of one that hands over the expressive obligation to mere speech whenever the composer feels inadequate to handle the dramatic line. It contains many tuneful and well-conceived set-pieces and also a great deal of carefully composed recitative. The transitions from speech to singing are ever so skillfully handled. The recitative itself, however, covers in most cases so wide a vocal range and is so heavily accompanied that it has to be sung fortissimo. It takes on, hence, a melodramatic quality not always appropriate to the verbal text, which is mostly quite simple conversation; and it also loses, of necessity, that verbal clarity that is recitative's chief beauty.

The music's most sophisticated aspect is its characterization of persons. Also, the elaboration of its musical ironies and cross-references is evidence of Mr. Blitzstein's penetrating mind. This is no banal love-me-love-my-tune music. It is dramatic comment of a high order. However, as usually happens with scores of predominantly ironical character, it tends to go a little bland when simple sentiment is its subject.

Rhythmically it did not seem to me structurally adequate, though this weakness may have come partly from the conducting. Time after time, energizing the metrics of a vocal line became the responsibility of the singing actor, the orchestra merely following him instead of carrying forward the composition.

In general, I should say, an undue dramatic obligation is placed on the singers. They are made to shout for minutes on end in the chest register of the speaking voice just before singing an aria. And since the music stops for quite long intervals, the pacing of the work cannot be controlled from the pit and falls to the singers, too. It is no wonder that the performance takes on early a hectic, a hysterical quality, loses musical tone, and fails to achieve musical shape. The piece has power, and some of this comes from the musical setting; but it remains in your reporter's mind a work of incomplete musical responsibility.

November 1, 1949

Pathos and the Macabre

THE CONSUL, musical play by GIAN-CARLO MENOTTI; first New York performance last night in the Ethel Barrymore Theater. The cast:

John Sorel	*Cornell MacNeil*
Magda Sorel	*Patricia Neway*
The Mother	*Marie Powers*
Chief Police Agent	*Leon Lishner*
First Police Agent	*Chester Watson*
Second Police Agent	*Donald Blackey*
The Secretary	*Gloria Lane*
Mr. Kofner	*George Jongeyans*
The Foreign Woman	*Maria Mario*
Anna Gomez	*Maria Andreassi*
Vera Boronell	*Lydia Summers*
Nika Magadoff	*Andrew McKinley*
Assan	*Francis Monachino*
Voice on the Record	*Mabel Mercer*

Conductor, LEHMAN ENGEL; stage director, Mr. MENOTTI. Settings designed by HORACE ARMISTEAD; costumes by GRACE HOUSTON.

The Consul is all Gian-Carlo Menotti's—the play, the music, the casting, the stage direction—a one-man music drama concentrated and powerful. To report on it as merely a piece of music would give no idea of its real nature. To recount it as drama would not explain its intensity. It is a play of horror and deep pathos, but these qualities in it are as much a result of musical stylization as they are of dramatic exposition.

It is musical investiture, with all the stiffness of stage movement that this involves, that has allowed the author to point up the story with irony and with a comic relief that in any realistic presentation would have been offensive to taste. Also, the story might have come out weak, from the very concentration of its appeal to pity, in a more straightforward telling. All the theater conventions, indeed— prose speech, rhyme, instrumental music, song, recitative, and choreography—have combined to give that story breadth of appeal and emotional perspective.

The musical score is apt and ever illustrative. Also, it is valuable to the narrative through its sustained emotional plan. Harmonically it is a bit chromatic and fussy, melodically a shade undistinguished. Constant undecisive modulation and the insistent repetition of melodic fragments tantalize the listener more than they satisfy musically. Recitative passages, however, are so skillfully set as to be almost unnoticeable, to provoke no listener resistance to this most perilous of all opera conventions. And the music of orchestral commentary is everywhere inventive and a help. The two big solos, a lullaby and a denunciation scene, are valuable to the play's progress and emphasis, but musically not very memorable.

The most striking and original musico-dramatic effect in the whole spectacle is the final scene, a fifteen-minute suicide by gas. Here the orchestra and choreographer take over, though there is some singing too. A vision of death beyond the threshold, set to a waltz in coffin clothes, brings the play to a moving end by exploiting in the most daring manner Mr. Menotti's gift for combining the macabre with the pathetic. A nightmare scene in the second act and a hypnotist's trick on the customers waiting in the office of the consulate had prepared stylistically this finale. All the same, it is as surprising as it is brilliant and vigorous, the most hair-raising among the many virtuoso theatrical effects that the author's fancy has conceived.

In a cast notable for musical excellence Patricia Neway, as the wife of a Resistance hero, stands out as a singing actress of unusual power. Marie Powers, the Mother, though satisfactory, is less impressive. Gloria Lane, the consulate secretary, is thoroughly pleasing in every way. All the men are good, and so are the singers of secondary roles. Lehman Engel, at the conductor's desk, produces sound orchestral balances, impeccable pacing of the whole, and unfailing dramatic animation. *The Consul* is a music drama of great power in a production remarkably efficient. I doubt if it makes musical history. but the musical elements contribute in a major way to a spectacle that may well have its place in our century's history of the stage. Mr. Menotti, though not quite a first-class composer, is surely

a bold, an original dramatic author. And music is the language
that he writes his dramas in.

March 17, 1950

The Met and the City Center

The seasonal closing of our two chief operatic establishments has
left pleasant memories of both. There has been, indeed, a goodly
number of uncommonly good opera performances at both houses.
And if certain off nights have seemed lacking in spark or in the
ultimate refinements, others have been thoroughly musical, animated,
communicative.

The Metropolitan has given us a revived *Simon Boccanegra* by
Verdi and a new production of Moussorgsky's *Khovantchina*. Both
were musically sumptuous and careful. Both are works of the highest
musical value; and both are, relatively speaking, novelties. The
former, we are told, will stay in repertory next year. The latter, it
seems, will not, though surely it is to be hoped that so noble a piece
will not go to storage for long. The Metropolitan's glory is its
ability to perform difficult and complex works. *Khovantchina* is one
of the grander monuments of music's history. It needs the kind of
grandiose production that only the Met can give; and we, the public,
need to hear it more frequently than has been formerly our privilege.

The City Center Opera Company has kept in the spring repertory
its excellent production of last fall, Prokofiev's *The Love for Three
Oranges*, and given us a new one, Puccini's *Turandot*. Both have
delighted the public. Both are distinguished· works. And both are a
welcome refreshment to repertory. Both works, of course, are over
twenty-five years old. Both houses have been reluctant to offer
operas, either foreign or domestic, of recent composition.

Operas 81

Opera at the City Center is a genuinely charming entertainment. The price is not high; tickets, with a little forethought, can be had; the productions are agreeable; the audience is lively. Almost any evening spent there is a rewarding one. The Metropolitan is expensive, difficult to get into, and not much fun except for the music. One is exigent about a show under those conditions. When something costs all that money and trouble (including often scalpers' prices, too), we expect of the performance nothing less than perfection. Musical inefficiencies that we condone at the City Center are not forgiven to the Met. When a Metropolitan performance is really good it is unforgettable. Perfection attained is no end impressive. But perfection missed is never a lively spectacle.

The City Center, with no such high-flown role to play, has no such disappointment to offer. Its excellences, ever a welcome surprise, provoke feelings of gratitude and warmth. Warmth, indeed, is felt constantly at this house. It is the tone of the audience. No such public, with its eagerness, liveness, cultural awareness, and quick-to-applaud friendliness, is elsewhere available in New York. It is as delightful a part of the show as the show itself. The City Center public is aware of quality and grateful for it. Since quality is abundant in the musical productions, the house is ever alert, happy, full of excitement. Any failure to achieve quality is quickly forgotten in the joy that accompanies its recognition in some other element of the performance.

It must be a pleasure for artists to work before such an audience. Certainly it is a pleasure to be part of that audience. The present writer finds at the City Center, moreover, a kind of opera production that he has always held in deep affection, a kind represented in Europe by the municipal establishments of Nice, Marseille, Strasbourg, Bordeaux, and some of the north Italian cities. The aim is quality and taste at the highest level attainable under the circumstances, and the amount of quality offered is invariably a money's worth.

Operas presented in this way often tell their story more vividly than when treated as vehicles for great vocalism and star conducting. These latter elements, when perfect, are a show in themselves.

Occasionally, just occasionally, they light up the score. When this miracle occurs, all the establishments pretending to absolute excellence are for one evening justified. The rest of the time they are pretty oppressive.

The municipal establishments do not fly so high or fall so dismally. They hedge-hop happily. The City Center has proved, moreover, with its ballet company, that its audience is thoroughly receptive to contemporary music and contemporary aesthetic conceptions. It can succeed with many an advanced work that might be risky for the Met. The latter can produce complex and difficult works with dignity and high musical power, but ever the success of the operation is precarious. The City Center gives opera at a price available to all and in a manner eminently acceptable, charming, graceful. Also, its performances seem always to have as their theme the work performed rather than the cast performing it. It makes no money, loses no money, asks no contributions, gives a wonderful show. No competitor to the Met at all, it is one of the most valued and valuable cultural institutions in a city rich in cultural offerings of every kind.

May 7, 1950

IV. STRICTLY OF THIS CENTURY

Glorious Loudness

PHILHARMONIC-SYMPHONY ORCHESTRA, LEOPOLD STOKOWSKI, conductor, concert last night in Carnegie Hall. Assisting choruses: SCHOLA CANTORUM, WESTMINSTER CHOIR, and boys' chorus from Public School No. 12, Manhattan.

In Ecclesiis Benedicite Domino from *Symphoniae Sacrae,* for two
    four-part choruses, organ, and brass   GIOVANNI GABRIELI
            (First Philharmonic-Symphony performance)
SYMPHONY NO. 8, IN E MAJOR, for orchestra, chorus, and soloists   MAHLER
            (First Philharmonic-Symphony performance)
    Soloists: Frances Yeend, soprano (Magna Peccatrix); Uta Graf, soprano

84

(Gretchen) ; Camilla Williams, soprano (Mater Gloriosa) ; Martha Lipton, contralto (Mulier Samaritana) ; Louise Bernhardt, contralto (Maria Aegyptiaca) ; Eugene Conley, tenor (Doctor Marianus) ; Carlos Alexander, baritone (Pater Ecstaticus) ; George London, bass (Pater Profundus).

Gustav Mahler's Eighth Symphony, as directed last night by Leopold Stokowski in Carnegie Hall, was a glorious experience to one who had not heard it before. Its sculpture of vast tonal masses at the end of each of the two movements was handled by the conductor in so noble a manner that the sound achieved monumentality while remaining musical. The effect was unquestionably grand.

The whole work, indeed, has grandeur and humility. In its eighty minutes of execution time no touch of the meretricious mars its devotional concentration on the meaning of its texts. These are two, the Latin hymn *Veni Creator Spiritus* and the last scene (in German) from Goethe's *Faust*. The symphony holds together as a musical piece and expresses its author's deepest religious impulses, as well as cultural convictions. A master workman, he gave to this work his utmost of seriousness and inspiration. It is a statue to his memory, if not his finest music.

Both as music and as a monument it is weakened by its melodic material, which is banal. Also by its harmony, which, though structurally adequate, is timid, unoriginal, unexpressive. The orchestral writing is ingenious, as always, though lacking somewhat in color for so long a piece; and the handling of the huge choral masses is both firm and delicate. The solo parts are lovely, too, as vocal writing. What the work lacks is melodic point, sharpness of outline. Weak thematic material, developed beyond its natural strength, becomes repetitive, loses communicative power. The last five minutes contain a real tune. The rest, for all the thought and skill involved in its composition, is pretty amorphous.

Some of this amorphousness comes from the composer's basic aesthetic assumption. This assumption, derived from the Finale of Beethoven's Ninth Symphony, seems to be that it is possible to make an artistically perfect work of music that will combine in equal proportions the symphony and the oratorio (or cantata). No such work has yet been produced. Even the Beethoven movement has never been universally voted by musicians to be successful. I do not think Mahler's Eighth is successful, either. It is not, in my estimate of it, a pure crystal. It is ambitious and sincere, and it has character. But its grandeur lies in certain skillful handlings and in the conception. It does not permeate the piece, which is soft inside.

One is grateful to Mr. Stokowski and to his assembled forces for letting us hear it. Also for giving it to us with such great care for musical decorum. Such handsome loudnesses as took place in both perorations one does not encounter often in a lifetime. The soloists were excellent too. It was a glorious performance of a noble but not wholly satisfactory work.

April 7, 1950

In Waltz Time

PHILHARMONIC-SYMPHONY ORCHESTRA, DIMITRI MITROPOULOS, conductor, concert last night in Carnegie Hall. Soloist, JOSEPH SZIGETI, Violinist.

OVERTURE to *The Marriage of Figaro*	MOZART
FIVE ORCHESTRAL PIECES	SCHÖNBERG
SYMPHONY IN E FLAT, No. 3, *Rhenish*	SCHUMANN
VIOLIN CONCERTO IN D MAJOR	BRAHMS

Arnold Schönberg's Five Orchestral Pieces, which Dimitri Mitropoulos conducted at last night's concert of the Philharmonic-Symphony Orchestra in Carnegie Hall, were written in 1909, nearly forty years ago. Previously they have been played in New York, I believe, one and three-fifths times. They are among the more celebrated works of our century, and yet few musicians or music lovers have heard them. The present writer, though the owner of a printed orchestral score for twenty-five years, listened to them last night with a virgin ear. Having followed the performance score in hand, he is able to certify that Mr. Mitropoulos and the Philharmonic boys read them to perfection and faithfully. His opinion of the work is that it deserves every bit of its world-wide prestige and none of its world-wide neglect.

The orchestral sound of the work is derived from French Impressionism in general and from the music of Debussy in particular. The orchestra is delicate, coloristic, and clean, at no point emphatic or demagogic. There is not in it one doubling of a note for purposes of weight. Harmonically the work is dissonant and atonal, though there is no twelve-tone row in it. Contrapuntally and rhythmically its texture resembles that of the Brahms Intermezzi, though it offers a more advanced state of the technique.

That technique tends toward fragmentation of the musical material through rhythmic and contrapuntal device. Schönberg here carries it close to the state of ultimate pulverization that his pupil Anton Webern achieved fifteen years later. Rhythmic contradictions, the gasping, almost fainting utterance of intense emotion in short phrases conventional of curve, the chromatic character of these phrases—all this is out of Brahms, though the harmony is far harsher and the sound of it all, orchestrally, is French.

The expressive character of the Five Pieces is deeply sentimental, in spite of a touch (and more) of irony. Four of the five are in triple time. Composed, as they are, almost wholly of phrases consecrated by Vienna to waltz usage, your reviewer is inclined to consider them a sort of apotheosis of the waltz. He realizes that their waltz structure is no obvious or perhaps even consciously intended communication. All the same, except for the one called "The Changing Chord" (in reality an unchanging one), which is an essay in pure orchestration, he finds them evocative of waltz moods and waltz textures, an etherealization of a theme that is at bottom just good old Vienna. He also suspects that in another decade they may be understood by all as something like that.

The rest of the program was carefully executed, a little dry, perhaps, but very neat, very pretty as workmanship and only occasionally a bit loud.

October 22, 1948

Star Dust and Spun Steel

PHILHARMONIC-SYMPHONY ORCHESTRA, DIMITRI MITROPOULOS, conductor, concert last night in Carnegie Hall. Soloist, ROBERT CASADESUS, pianist.

OVERTURE to *Anacreon*	CHERUBINI
PIANO CONCERTO NO. 5, IN E FLAT, *Emperor*	BEETHOVEN
SYMPHONY	WEBERN
(First Philharmonic-Symphony performance)	
SYMPHONIC DANCES, OP. 45	RACHMANINOFF

Anton Webern's Symphony for chamber orchestra, the novelty of last night's Philharmonic concert in Carnegie Hall, was "advanced" music when first played here twenty years ago; and it still is. For all the world-wide spread of the twelve-tone technique that has taken place since then, it would be hard to find today five living adepts of it whose writing is so firm and so sophisticated as Webern's was. The audience effect of this work attested also to its vitality. Not only were repeated bows taken by the conductor, Dimitri Mitropoulos, and his excellent musicians. There was actually booing in the hall, a phenomenon almost unknown at the Philharmonic.

The piece itself offends, as it delights, by its delicacy, transparency, and concentration. The first movement, for all its canonic rigor, is something of an ultimate in pulverization—star dust at the service of sentiment. Each instrument plays just one note, at most two; then another carries on the theme. The theme itself is a row of tones isolated from one another by scale skips. The texture is thin, too. One note at a time, just occasionally two or three, is the rule of its instrumental utterance. And yet the piece has a melodic and an expressive consistency. It is clearly about something and under no temptation to fidget. Its form, I may add, is roughly that of a binary, or Scarlatti-type sonata; and its rhythmic pulse, save for a few retards in the second movement, is steady.

This movement (there are only two) is a set of variations on the work's whole twelve-tone row, first stated completely at this point.

Rhythm is broken up into asymmetrical fragments. The melodic pulverization is less fine, however, than that of the first movement. Occasionally an instrument will articulate as many as eight or ten notes at a stretch. Some of these are even repeated notes. Metrical fragmentation has taken the place of melodic. The sonorous texture becomes even thinner at the end than anything one has heard previously. A tiny sprinkle of sounds; two widely spaced ones on the harp; and vaporization is complete.

There is every reason to believe the Philharmonic's reading of this tiny but ever so tough work to have been correct. Musicians following the score could question only the size, here and there, of some minute crescendo. The rendering was clear, clean, tonally agreeable, and expressive. Expressive of exactly what, would be difficult to say, as it is of any work. Nevertheless, consistency and self-containment, ever the signs of expressive concentration, were present to the ear, just as they are to the eye reading the score. Once again there was cause to be grateful to Mr. Mitropoulos for his assiduity toward neglected distinction and for his enormous loyalty to the text of a work rare, complex, and in every way difficult.

The rest of the program, standard stuff, sounded gross beside Webern's spun steel. Robert Casadesus played a Beethoven concerto in businesslike fashion, with dispatch and efficiency. A Rachmaninoff piece gave the conductor the conventional odds. Only the Cherubini overture, *Anacreon,* long absent from programs, reminded us that ancient springs can still run fresh when overuse ceases to pollute them. It also reminded us that Rossini's much-admired lively spirits were not so much a personal gift as a heritage from predecessors and fellow countrymen, from this one in particular. A jolly piece and a shapely one by the founder of French musical pedagogy.

January 27, 1950

Gloomy Masterpiece

PHILHARMONIC-SYMPHONY ORCHESTRA, DIMITRI MITROPOULOS, conductor, concert last night in Carnegie Hall. Soloist, JOSEPH SZIGETI, violinist.

OVERTURE to *Der Freischütz*	WEBER
VIOLIN CONCERTO IN G MINOR	BACH
VIOLIN CONCERTO	BERG
(First Philharmonic-Symphony performance)	
SYMPHONY NO. 4, IN F MINOR	VAUGHAN WILLIAMS

The star of last night's Philharmonic program was the late Alban Berg, author of the violin concerto played by Joseph Szigeti. Mr. Szigeti himself, who also played a Bach concerto (the G minor), and the other composers represented all fitted modestly into a background for this striking work. Only Dimitri Mitropoulos, who conducted, stuck out a bit. Apparently in one of his febrile moods, he kept getting between each work and its rendering, standing out against it, till closing the eyes, with all the risks of somnolence entailed, became the only escape. Even then one could not avoid an awareness that everything was being overplayed, overpushed, overdramatized, overexpressed. Everything, at least, but the Berg Concerto, itself so powerful, so lucid an introspection that even a tortured and twisting conductor could not overshadow its gloom.

Expressionismus at its most intense and visceral is the work's aesthetic. The twelve-tone-row technique is the method beneath its coherence. Pure genius is the source of its strength. Somber of coloration, its sound is dominated ever by the soloist, the string section, and the horns. Based on a row that begins with a circle of fifths, the constant recurrence of this easily noticed progression brings some monotony to the texture. Expressive chiefly of basic pleasure-pain and tension-relief patterns (the reason for my calling its expression visceral), its few cerebral references (to a Viennese waltz in the first movement and to a Bach chorale in the last) stand out like broken memories in a delirium.

The piece is too continuous, of course, too consistent to represent mind-wandering. It is a work of art, not a madman's dream, though its gloom is almost too consistent to be real. Nevertheless, it would not be fair to suspect a piece clearly so inspired in musical detail of essential second-rateness. One must, I think, take it or leave it as a whole. Your reviewer has long been willing to take it, to enjoy its musical fancy and to admire its coloristic intensities, without, however, at any time finding his emotions transported. Such an experience often accompanies the hearing of works removed from one's personal sensibilities by space and time. It does not prove a thing against a masterpiece.

Alban Berg is dead; he has joined the classic masters. One does not have to vote about his work, to love it or to hate it. It exists in perfection, for whatever use we may care to make of it. I suspect that the world will be making more and more use of this particular piece. And I believe strongly that Mr. Mitropoulos has rendered the music world a service by providing on this occasion (as on a previous one back in 1945, when he led it in a broadcast N.B.C. concert) auditory access to it. So has Mr. Szigeti by playing the solo part so manfully on both occasions. I suspect that the trouble with the rest of the evening came from the conductor's devotion to the Berg Concerto. He seemed to have got by means of it into a state of intensity, almost of sanctification, that rubbed off on everything else. It did the other works little good, as you may imagine.

December 16, 1949

The Ultimate of Lucidity

N.B.C. Symphony Orchestra, Ernest Ansermet, conductor, concert broadcast Saturday evening between 6:30 and 7:30 from National Broadcasting Company's Studio 8-H, Rockefeller Center.

Paraphrase on a Chorale from Hassler, for strings	Templeton Strong
Jeux	Debussy
Symphony No. 5	Martinu

(American première)

Ernest Ansermet, conducting last Saturday afternoon's concert of the N.B.C. Symphony Orchestra in Studio 8-H, Radio City, gave us two works virtually unknown to New York listeners and one brand-new one. He also showed us the conductor's art at a degree of mastery rarely to be encountered, even in these days. The works were beautiful and their readings perfection. The orchestra itself, which varies in efficiency from week to week, like any other guest-conducted ensemble, gave out on this occasion sounds to remind us all that its executant personnel is that of a great orchestra.

The string section was shown us in glory by means of a Paraphrase on a Chorale by Leo Hassler. The chorale is the Good Friday one, *O Sacred Head Now Wounded*. The composer of the work is the aged Templeton Strong, an American long resident in Switzerland. The style of the paraphrase is derived from Bach's chorale-preludes by way of Romantic modulation. It is tasteful, touching, and skillfully written, if not unusually original. The pleasure of hearing it was double, because it is intrinsically a far from stupid piece and because the N.B.C. strings are among the finest in America.

Bohuslav Martinu's Fifth Symphony, which ended the program, an American première, shows this living master at his highest point, for the present, of originality and freedom. Martinu is clearly, as of today, a symphonist. He moves in the form with ease, makes it speak for him. This symphony speaks in double-talk, says always two things at once. Almost nowhere else in the music of our time is antiphony, both of sound and of sense, so constantly present. The tunes, the counterpoint, the harmony of this work are personal and expressive. Its shape is plain and free, without any looseness. Its speech is noble, without any demagoguery or any pretentiousness. Others have used the symphony for its prestige, for its box-office power, or for private musical ends. To Martinu alone among contemporary masters has it been given to elevate the symphonic tone.

Debussy's ballet *Jeux* (or *Games*), written in 1912 and produced by Diaghilev in 1913 (the scenarist and choreographer, Nijinsky, also dancing the male role), has long been neglected by conductors, even in France. The last orchestral work to be fully orchestrated by Debussy himself, it represents at its ultimate that tendency toward the attenuation of musical materials into a luminous and golden dust, of which *La Mer* and *Images* are earlier examples. It glows like mercury vapor or a sunset in Texas and is as immaterial to the touch. Sonorously it is a piece for two harps, four flutes, and subdivided strings, in which the rest of its large orchestra merely amplifies climactically the basic coloration. Expressively it is an apotheosis of the waltz. Formally it is a masterpiece of continuity that employs no classical continuity device for its own sake but that holds together in the most surprising way. Its musical language, starting out with twelve-tone chords and continuing to the end in polyharmony and polyrhythm, achieves an effect close to atonality and remains today advanced.

Jeux is a unique work, an ultimate work, an end, and maybe a beginning. Executed with Mr. Ansermet's equally unique and ultimate lucidity, it is also one of the most ravishing pieces imaginable. In hands less loving it might easily take on weight and fall apart. In his it is a lesson in how French music at its summit of achievement should, could, and must be made to sound. Mr. Ansermet himself, in case you haven't heard about him, is conductor of l'Orchestre de la Suisse Romande in Geneva and one of the half-dozen greatest living orchestral workmen and interpreters. He has two more Saturday concerts at N.B.C.

January 26, 1948

The Style Is the Subject

EVENING OF STRAVINSKY MUSIC, yesterday at Town Hall, with the Chamber Art Society, IGOR STRAVINSKY and ROBERT CRAFT conducting. Assisting pianist, ELLY KASSMAN.

Symphonies d'instruments à vent (1920, revised 1947), played twice, Mr. Stravinsky conducting. (First concert performances in revised version)
Danses Concertantes (1941), Mr. Stravinsky conducting.
CAPRICCIO FOR PIANO AND ORCHESTRA (1929); soloist, Miss Kassman, Mr. Craft conducting.
SYMPHONY IN C (1940). (First New York concert performance)

The musico-intellectual world turned out in considerable numbers for last night's concert in Town Hall of the Chamber Art Society. Igor Stravinsky's music and presence were the attraction. The program gave us four works rarely heard, covering a period of twenty years in the composer's middle and later middle life, from 1920 to 1941. Two of these, the *Symphonies of Wind Instruments,* from 1920, and the *Danses Concertantes,* of 1941, were conducted by himself. The Symphony in C, of 1940, and the Capriccio for Piano and Orchestra, of 1929, were led by Robert Craft. Elly Kassman played the solo part in the latter work. Execution throughout was excellent.

The wind piece, dedicated to the memory of Claude Debussy, was given in a recently made revision. Though it remains a striking piece chiefly for its dissonant and almost motionless chorale at the end, throughout it is a deeply expressive work in mortuary vein. The other pieces, neoclassic in character, are less directly expressive, being chiefly evocative of scenes, periods, and circumstances from the history of musical composition.

The Capriccio, derived from Weber's Konzertstück, is a brilliant potpourri of Schumann, Chopin, Liszt, Delibes, and probably some others. The *Danses Concertantes* evoke the ballet music of Adam in particular and of the mid-nineteenth century in general. The Symphony in C is modeled after the Viennese classical works in that form, after Haydn, Mozart, and the early Beethoven.

94

The Symphony is the noblest of the three works, by its grandly simple material, its shapeliness, and its elevated tone. The others are a bit frivolous, though plenty of fun, and more than a little discontinuous. Even the Symphony falls apart a bit in the last movement. All the same, it is a handsome piece, as the Capriccio is a jolly and brilliant one and the *Danses Concertantes* an attractive one for anybody who likes to get sentimental about the ballet.

Stravinsky's neoclassic music having never had a real audience success, as his Impressionistic early theater works have had, his friends and disciples tend to defend it as a cause rather than to discriminate one piece of it from another. Last night's concert gave us a chance, however, to do just that by providing three celebrated and varied examples of it in a row. My choice among these, if I must make one, is the Symphony in C. Another's will be the Capriccio or the *Danses*. The attractiveness of Stravinsky's whole neoclassic production lies, however, less in the expressive power of a given work than in the musical language in which they are all written.

This is a compound of grace and of brusqueness thoroughly Russian in its charm and its rudeness and so utterly sophisticated intellectually that few musicians of intellectual bent can resist it. The general public has never cared much about modern neoclassicism, but does listen to it more easily than it used to. I don't think musical ticket buyers are overfond of indirectness, and certainly most of anybody's neoclassic works are indirect. Every now and then, however, one of them forgets its game of reminding you about the history of music and starts saying things of its own. To me the Symphony in C does that, just as the wind instrument *Symphonies*, on the whole an inferior work but not an eclectic or derivative one, have always done.

April 12, 1948

Joan of Arc in Close-Up

PHILHARMONIC-SYMPHONY ORCHESTRA, CHARLES MUNCH, conductor, assisted by the Westminster Choir, Dr. JOHN FINLEY WILLIAMSON, director, first performance in the United States of the dramatic oratorio *Jeanne d'Arc au Bûcher* (Joan of Arc at the Stake), text by PAUL CLAUDEL, music by ARTHUR HONEGGER, last night in Carnegie Hall.

Speaking roles: *Vera Zorina* as Jeanne; *Raymond Gerome* as Frère Dominique.
Singing roles: *Nadine Conner* as the Virgin; *Jarmila Novotna* as Marguerite; *Enid Szantho* as Catherine; *Joseph Laderoute* as a Voice; *Jean de Luxembourg* and *Regnault de Chartres* as Porcus and First Herald; *Lorenzo Alvary* as Guillaume de Flavy, a Voice, and Second Herald.

The performance itself was perfection, that of Honegger's *Joan of Arc at the Stake,* as given at last night's Philharmonic concert in Carnegie Hall under the direction of Charles Munch. Orchestra, chorus, and soloists (as listed above) did everything convincingly, musically just right. And everybody's French was excellent.

The piece itself is what the French call a "big machine"—a work of some musical and literary pretentions set for orchestra, chorus, soloists, and speaking voice. The inventor of the formula, so far as I know, is Berlioz. Its local version is the Norman-Corwin-style radio number. Its most successful European practitioners, among the living, are Arthur Honegger, who composed the present score, and Paul Claudel, author of the present text.

Joan at the Stake aims to please all, save possibly the Marxian Left, by exploiting religious and patriotic sentiments without doctrinal precision. It appeals to the theater instinct in us all by the realistic evocation of horror scenes. It appeases the lover of modern music with bits of polytonal composition. It impresses all by its elaborate mobilization of musical effectives. It offers, in short, virtually everything a concert can offer but bets on nothing.

The weakness of the work lies exactly in its failure to bet, to make clear whether we are listening to a musical work on a literary text or to a literary work with musical commentary. The fact that the title role is a speaking role, not a singing one, is the chief source of this ambiguity. Another is the lack of musical shape in the set-pieces.

These are full of expressive variety and abundant of apt musical invention, but they are tied tightly to a text that has itself little of formal shape or progress. The music illustrates the text in running commentary but does not take it in hand, add unity and emphasis. As a result, the work makes rather the same effect that a film of the same length (seventy-five minutes) might. It is picturesque at all moments, varied, and vastly detailed; but it lacks the monumentality that its oratorio layout would seem to impose. It is all in close-ups. At no point do we get a panoramic view, an epic breadth in the narrative.

This is why, for all the fine fancy in Honegger's music, *Joan at the Stake* remains somewhat trivial. It is closer in feeling to devotional than to dramatic literature. It is like some garrulous meditation on the Stations of the Cross. Its convulsive tone is striking, but there is not the dignity in the whole conception that one might expect from a musician of world-wide prestige dealing with a subject so familiar, so touching, and so grand. The effort to please everybody possible in every possible way has left the whole effort touched with a flavor of insincerity, that same flavor we all know so well from our own "big machines" of radio and the films.

January 2, 1948

Handsome Period Pieces

FESTIVAL OF CONTEMPORARY FRENCH MUSIC presented by the JUIL-
LIARD SCHOOL OF MUSIC, second evening yesterday in the Juilliard
Concert Hall.

Entr'acte (1924): film by RENÉ CLAIR; score by ERIK SATIE; arranged for two
pianos by DARIUS MILHAUD and HENRY BRANT.
    Pianists, Frederic Cohen and Frederic Waldman
Le Bal Masqué: profane cantata for baritone and chamber ensemble (1932),
FRANCIS POULENC; text by MAX JACOB.
    Soloist, Warren Galjour; Frederic Waldman conducting
Le Pauvre Matelot: Lament in three acts; music by DARIUS MILHAUD; text by
JEAN COCTEAU; translation by LORRAINE NOEL FINEY. The cast: The Sailor,
Diran Akmajian; His Wife, *Geraldine Hamburg;* His Father-in-Law, *Edward
Ansara;* His Friend, *Lorenzo Malfatti.*
    Conductor, FREDERIC WALDMAN; stage director, FREDERIC COHEN; scenic
director, FREDERICK KIESLER.

Erik Satie's *Entr'acte,* which opened last night's program at the Juilliard School (the second in a series devoted to contemporary French
music), is, in the judgment of this reviewer, the finest film score
ever composed. The film itself, made by René Clair after a scenario
of Francis Picabia, is a brilliant piece of work but completely nowadays (if also delightfully) a period piece. Produced in 1924 as a
divertissement joining two scenes of a ballet, *Relâche* (composed
by Satie and decorated by Picabia), it takes us back to the still inno-
cent last days of Dada, before Surrealism had turned our fantasies
sour, sexy, and mean. It is not about anything at all but being young
and in Paris and loving to laugh, even at funerals. In those days
there was still comic cinema, too.

The excellence of the musical score composed to accompany this
otherwise silent film with real orchestral sounds (these were played
last night by two pianists) is due to Satie's having understood correctly the limitations and possibilities of a photographic narrative
as subject matter for music. Also to the durable nature of his musical invention. The whole is made out of short musical bits like build-
ing-blocks. These are neutral enough in character to accompany

appropriately many different scenes and images, but also interesting enough as music to bear repetition without fatigue to the listener. These musical blocks are organized into a rondo form as squarely terraced as a New York skyscraper and every bit as practical in function.

Satie's music for *Entr'acte*, consequently, is not only beautiful in itself. It is also efficient as expression; it is appropriate to the film. It avoids banality of sentiment by avoiding sentiment altogether, by keeping its expressivity objective, by never identifying itself with any person on the screen. By remaining ever as cool and clear as René Clair's photography itself, it remains also as clear in meaning and as satisfying intrinsically. I do not know another film score so durable, so distinguished.

Francis Poulenc's secular cantata *Le Bal Masqué*, on poems of the late Max Jacob, a piece in six sections for baritone and chamber orchestra, shows us a master of musical exuberance at the climax of his youthful period. It was composed in 1932, about the last year anybody in Europe was really carefree, and it is musical highjinks from beginning to end. Its *pasticcio* of urban banalities, melodic and rhythmic, is rendered personal and interesting by the extreme elegance of the vocal lines and instrumental textures. Thin, clean, brilliant, frank, and delicate, its charm, its good humor, its wit and poetry, like those of Satie himself (though the invention of it is less jewel-like and original than Satie's) are as fresh as the day the piece was written.

The Poulenc piece and Darius Milhaud's short opera *Le Pauvre Matelot*, to a text of Jean Cocteau, were conducted with taste and understanding by Frederic Waldman. The latter work, which I shall not review, because time presses and because it has been given before in New York, was decorated imaginatively by Frederick Kiesler. Neither work was as well projected vocally by the Juilliard students as they were instrumentally. The Poulenc cantata, from the latter point of view, was an impeccable execution. All three works were a pleasure to hear. Perhaps the Milhaud opera has aged a little; and certainly it always was, though largely composed of gay sailor chanteys like "Blow the Man Down," a shade lugubrious. Also a bit heavy in orchestral texture for its vocal line.

December 2, 1948

Religious Corn

PHILHARMONIC-SYMPHONY ORCHESTRA, LEOPOLD STOKOWSKI, conductor, concert Thursday night in Carnegie Hall. Soloist, WANDA LANDOWSKA, harpsichordist.

Offrande	AUBERT
(First performance in the United States)	
Concert Champêtre FOR HARPSICHORD AND ORCHESTRA	POULENC
Trois Petites Liturgies de la Présence Divine	MESSIAEN
(First performance in the United States)	
Women's Chorus of the Schola Cantorum	
HARPSICHORD CONCERTO IN B FLAT	HANDEL
SYMPHONY NO. 35, in D MAJOR (K. 385), *Haffner*	MOZART

Olivier Messiaen's *Three Short Liturgies of the Divine Presence*, which received their first American hearing Thursday night under the direction of Leopold Stokowski at a regular subscription concert of the Philharmonic-Symphony Orchestra in Carnegie Hall, were composed in 1944. The program notes of the occasion give their première date as 1946, and that is probably correct for public performance in a hall. Nevertheless, I reviewed them in this newspaper on September 23 of the previous year, my acquaintance being based on a recording made by the French National Radio from a broadcast performance that had taken place even earlier. The work has been known to musicians here and in Europe for some five years as its composer's most generally successful work in large form. By successful I mean both typical of his precedures and having a direct audience appeal.

100

Somehow a good deal of that appeal got lost Thursday night in the broad spaces of Carnegie Hall. Though small of instrumentation, the piece needs to sound loud and full and penetrating. Heard that way, its rhythmic and instrumental variety holds immediate attention. Heard at a distance, its trite melodic content and static structure dominate the effect. There is no question that this work is the product of a delicate ear and an ingenious musical mind. Its aesthetic value has not been entirely convincing to the purely musical world, though laymen have usually cast their vote in its favor. My own opinion is that its author is a case not unlike that of Scriabine. That is to say that he is a skilled harmonist and orchestrator, full of theories and animated by no small afflatus, but that there is a sticky syrup in his product which hinders its flow at concert temperatures.

The two composers have an identical preoccupation with ecstasy and an identical inability to keep a piece moving along. Their religious inspiration has no energizing force; it is druglike, pretty-pretty, hypnotic. In Messiaen's case all the paraphernalia of commercial glamour are mobilized to depict the soul in communion with God—a ladies' chorus, divided strings, piano, harp, celesta, vibraphone, Chinese cymbal, tamtam, and an electronic instrument playing vibrato (in this case the Ondes Martenot). The sounds of such an ensemble, however intelligently composed, cannot transport this listener much farther than the Hollywood cornfields. Placing them at the service of religion does not, in his experience, ennoble them; it merely reduces a pietistic conception of some grandeur to the level of the late Aimee Semple McPherson.

Framing this novelty, which for all its silliness is musically highly original, one heard twice the impeccable and ever wondrous Wanda Landowska. She gave us Poulenc's *Concert Champêtre* in its original form (for harpsichord with orchestra) and a Handel organ (or harpsichord) concerto too. Nothing banal, nothing unlovely marred her readings; and the seemingly frail instrument sounded forth with a lordly clang through the fine textures of both composers. Earlier there had been an *Offrande* by Louis Aubert, a short memorial work pleasingly sonorous but not in itself, I should think, memorable. Afterward came the Mozart *Haffner* Symphony. This last your reporter regretfully passed up, the hour being already past 10:30.

November 19, 1949

Thanksgiving Turkey

PHILHARMONIC-SYMPHONY ORCHESTRA, DIMITRI MITROPOULOS, conductor, concert last night in Carnegie Hall. Soloist, MISCHA ELMAN, violinist.

Le Chasseur Maudit	FRANCK
SYMPHONY NO. 4	ERNST KRENEK
(First performance)	
VIOLIN CONCERTO IN D MAJOR	TCHAIKOVSKY

Dimitri Mitropoulos conducted the Philharmonic last night at the regular subscription concert in Carnegie Hall in a way to make the heart rejoice. His work was the only unalloyed pleasure, however, that can be testified from this mourner's bench. César Franck's *Le Chasseur Maudit* is a harmless enough piece, all about what happens to people who go hunting on Sunday. And Mischa Elman, a ripe but still sound violinist, playing the Tchaikovsky Concerto, an overripe but still not wholly withered comestible, offers quiet entertainment for a Thanksgiving night.

Ernst Krenek's Symphony No. 4, a first performance, was the really indigestible dish. The style of this work, pan-diatonic neo-classicism, and the subject matter of it, an emulation of Beethoven's middle period, are familiar to all nowadays. They are the veriest routine of the conservatories. Mr. Krenek's high musical skill and serious aims are far from offensive, either. They are perhaps the leavening element, indeed, if any is present, in that sad cake. It is troublesome to encounter a work so seemingly serious in thought, so certainly ambitious, and so thoroughly well composed, in a practical sense, and yet to be utterly unable at any point to be convinced by it.

Perhaps the overweening ambition of it is what sinks it. The idea of making a symphony that shall be monumental, impressive, forcible, easy to understand, and at the same time of an impeccable modernism is not a new idea; but neither is it a very good one. It is not a good one because it starts with an effect that it is desired to achieve rather than with a real musical idea that it has become urgent to communicate. Sometimes, starting from such a program, a composer gets his ideas to flowing; and real music comes out after all. The depressing quality about Mr. Krenek's new symphony is that the author has carried out his admitted intention to the letter. He has produced, in consequence, a pseudo-masterpiece with about as much savor to it as a pasteboard turkey.

The presentation by Mr. Mitropoulos and the Philharmonic boys of this (in the Broadway sense) turkey lacked nothing as a professional performance. All was clear, smoothly turned out, equilibrated. The work itself, in no way difficult of comprehension, confused nobody. Anybody could see that it was as empty as it was handsome. Anybody could hear, too, that Mr. Mitropoulos, playing not matter what, is a musician of quality so distinguished that one scarcely minds his playing, as he so often does, no matter what. He rather enjoys, I think, animating dead turkeys.

November 28, 1947

Masterpieces Revived

THE NATIONAL ASSOCIATION FOR AMERICAN COMPOSERS AND CONDUCTORS, concert in Times Hall last night. Participants: MARTIN

ORENSTEIN, flute; LOUIS PAUL, clarinet; DAVID ABOSCH, oboe; PINSON BOBO, horn; MARK POPKIN, bassoon; WILLIAM ROSE, HERBERT WEKSELBLATT, tubas; The Riverside Quintet; ROBERT NAGEL, JAMES HUSTIS, trumpets; RANIER DE INTINIS, horn; ROBERT HALE, RICHARD HIXSON, RALPH JOSEPH, trombones; LOU HARRISON, conductor; SARA CARTER, soprano; DAVID GARVEY, pianist.

SUITE FOR WIND QUINTET	HENRY COWELL
PASTORALE FOR WIND QUINTET	VINCENT PERSICHETTI
QUINTET FOR WINDS	ELLIOTT CARTER
Even Though the World Keeps Changing; On Death;	
Sister Jane	DAVID DIAMOND
Sunset; Day	EUNICE LEA KETTERING
Let Us Walk in the White Snow	MARY HOWE
It Is So Long; For My Lady; Alleluia	EVERETT HELM
DUO FOR TUBAS	RICHARD FRANKO GOLDMAN
MUSIC FOR FIVE BRASS INSTRUMENTS	INGOLF DAHL
Angels	CARL RUGGLES

Carl Ruggles's *Angels* was the high point of the concert presented last night in Times Hall by the National Association for American Composers and Conductors. Other works had elegance or musical distinction, and all were handsomely executed. But Ruggles's piece is a masterpiece and one almost wholly unknown today. Its revival after more than twenty years was accompanied by the kind of intellectual excitement that has ever attended its performance, plus the deep joy of the young just making its discovery.

Angels is part of a longer work entitled *Men and Angels*, composed in 1921. This section, as rescored in 1938, is a sustained and tranquil motet for four trumpets and three trombones, all muted. The texture of it is chromatic secundal counterpoint. Its voices, nondifferentiated as to expressive function, are woven together by thematic imitation. The dissonance-tension is uniform throughout, hence, in the long run, harmonious, though that tension carries the maximum of dissonance possible to seven voices. Complete avoidance of the dramatic and the picturesque gives to the work a simplicity and a nobility rare in the music of our time. Its plain nobility of expression and the utter perfection of its work-

104

manship place Ruggles as one of our century's masters, perhaps the one among all from whom the young have most to learn just now.

Preceding this extraordinary and secretly powerful work, there had taken place a concert of music for wind instruments, including the human voice, the only exception being a pianoforte, played ever so beautifully by David Garvey to accompany the singer. Most impressive among these works, to your reporter, was a Quintet for Winds by Elliott Carter, a solid work with musical interest in it and weight in the expression. A Duo in three movements for two bass tubas, by Richard Franko Goldman, had naturally a certain comic charm and surprisingly both musical grace and sweetness of sound. It was soft, velvet-footed, and in every way delicately pleasing.

The rest of the program was agreeable but not particularly fresh, excepting for one delicious Chorale movement in Henry Cowell's Suite for Wind Quintet. Vincent Persichetti's Pastorale for the same group showed fancy but was loosely held together. Ingolf Dahl's Music for Five Brass Instruments, an ambitious work in three extended movements, is more worthy than original of thought. Among the songs, all had quality but none, I think, a completely sustained inspiration.

The wind players, all Juilliard students, had been trained by Richard Franko Goldman; and genuinely fine they were for technical excellence and musical understanding. Sara Carter, soprano, did well by the songs. Lou Harrison conducted Ruggles's *Angels* reverently, admirably. It was a lovely concert, in every way out of the ordinary; and Ruggles's piece is great music.

February 28, 1949

Yesterday's Modernism

LEAGUE OF COMPOSERS, program dedicated to PAUL ROSENFELD, last night in the Museum of Modern Art.

SONATA FOR OBOE AND PIANO	CHARLES MILLS
Melvin Kapp and Sylvan Fox	
THREE MOODS	LEO ORNSTEIN
Grant Johannesen, pianist	
DUO FOR VIOLIN AND PIANO	ROGER SESSIONS
Nicolai Berezowsky and Donald Kemp	
SIX PALESTINIAN SONGS	STEPHAN WOLPE

Arline Carmen, mezzo-soprano; Leon Lishner, baritone; Irma Wolpe, pianist

CONCERTO FOR STRING QUARTET, PIANO, AND CLARINET   ROY HARRIS
    Richard Adams and Emma Jo McCracken, violinists; Gabriel Gruber, violist; Charles McCracken, cellist; Herbert Tichman, clarinetist; Joseph Bloch, pianist.

Hyperprism   EDGAR VARÈSE
        Ensemble of twenty-four conducted by Frederic Waldman

The League of Composers concert, which took place last night in the Museum of Modern Art, lasted till eleven o'clock; and your reviewer, the night being rainy, did not reach his desk till fifteen minutes later. Consequently, in order to cover a concert of some intellectual importance, he is going to take the liberty of stating his judgments in summary, stenographic fashion. But first it must be listed that all the executions were excellent, unusually distinguished being the piano playing of Grant Johannesen, the violin playing of Nikolai Berezowsky, and the singing of Arline Carmen. Especial thanks are due also to Frederic Waldman, who conducted the Varèse piece perfectly, at least to these ears.

The Varèse work, entitled *Hyperprism*, is real "modern music" of twenty years back; and it still makes its point. That point is that beauty does not require cantilena, harmony, contrapuntal imitation, or deliberate pathos. It can be made with elements commonly considered to be noise, and it does not even have to confine its sound sources to the conventionally ignoble. Trumpets, trombones, flutes, horns, piccolos, and the classical instruments of percussion give out purer sounds than flower pots and brakebands. Consequently they are useful. But out with their sentimental connotations! They are there as sound sources, not as poetic references.

The sounds that Varèse makes in this piece are handsome in the abstract. Their composition is rhythmically interesting, moreover; and with no cue as to the work's particular meaning, your listener found it absorbing, convincing, beautiful, and in every way grand. That the League of Composers, which fought this composer bitterly and all too successfully twenty years back, should revive him now is poetic justice. Let no one think, however, that they have just made his acquaintance or that they are recalling any historical benefaction of theirs.

As recalling former successes of the modern-music movement, the League gave us last night three jolly pieces by Leo Ornstein, from 1916, rhythmically thoroughly alive, if harmonically nothing difficult. Three piano pieces by Roger Sessions, though harmonically sophisticated, were as dead as the day of their birth. Roy Harris's Concerto for String Quartet, Clarinet and Piano, is still, twenty years later, real chamber music, with no more faults than are to be found in Brahms and with all the virtues. And Stephan Wolpe's songs, the evening's only first performance, are knockouts in the vein of yesterday's modernism and up to date in their use of Hebraic texts, references to Israel being the last word today in successful public relations. They are really quite good songs, but so are Ornstein's pieces good piano music. It was hard to know, indeed, among all these period-style compositions, exactly where real quality lay, excepting for the Varèse work, which, by any standards I know, is great music.

January 24, 1949

Five Symphonies

One of the striking characteristics of contemporary musical modernism is a tendency on the part of composers to write symphonies. The
heroes and founding fathers did no such thing. Not Richard Strauss
or Satie or Debussy or Ravel ever touched the form for its own sake,
and Stravinsky's early student piece of that title was long viewed
by his friends as a youthful indiscretion. The pupils of César Franck,
conservative modernists, did write them—d'Indy and Chausson
and Dukas and d'Indy's pupil Albert Roussel. But the composers
who really forged the modern language stuck pretty consistently
to objective expression and avoided the formally introspective.
Even Debussy, who invented in the last decade of his life our
century's characteristic form of neoclassicism, carried its aesthetic
no farther in his three sonatas than an evocation of historic textures. Expansion of the ego, à la Beethoven, was generally considered in the advanced music world that preceded World War I as
an unworthy source of inspiration and reactionary.

After 1918 the whole advanced world went a little reactionary,
however, and began to work at the abstract forms that for two centuries had provided vessels for musical private thoughts. First the
fugue was restored to favor and then the symphony. Milhaud,
Honegger, Hindemith, and Prokofiev approached the latter with cir-
cumspection through the concerto, the string quartet, and the sonata.
So did Stravinsky and Ravel and Schönberg. The last two never wrote
an orchestral work of that title; but Stravinsky has followed his
younger colleagues in their dangerous path; and nowadays every
child in a conservatory, or just out of one, will write you a symphony with no more sense of sin than he would have in taking a
highball.

There remains, however, a marked difference among modern composers in the way they approach the form. The Soviet Russians
use it for impersonal editorial ends (à la Brahms). The Central
Europeans impersonate oratory with it, also à la Brahms. The
French stick close to landscape, as Berlioz did. The Americans, and

this includes Europeans long resident here, Stravinsky and Milhaud and Hindemith and Krenek and Tansman, mostly follow the Viennese masters. So do the English, excepting Vaughan Williams, a pupil of Ravel, who preserves an almost Impressionistic, or at least Mendelssohnian, relation to landscape painting.

When I say that Stravinsky and Milhaud, for all their training in landscape and the picturesque, follow a Viennese model when composing symphonies, I mean simply that, like Beethoven, they are preoccupied with making a familiar form expressive. The French of France, on the other hand, are more likely to start from an expressive concept and to use familiar form as merely an expedient for sustaining length and emphasis, much as Richard Strauss did long ago in his Sinfonia Domestica. Even their titles betray this difference. Our local writers give their symphonies numbers. Honegger calls his also *Liturgical* or *The Delights of Basel*. Rosenthal calls his most recent *Christmas Symphonies* and adds a precise description of each movement's pictorial content. Antheil, Cowell, Copland, Piston, Schuman, Harris, Ives—the Americans in general —offer no explanation. When they do, in program notes, they make a strictly formal analysis and insist that any resemblance to real persons or places is accidental.

Five notable new symphonies have come to my ears this season in New York and its environs. Locally we have heard Honegger's Fourth (*Deliciae Baslerienses*) and Antheil's Fifth. I heard Rosenthal's *Christmas Symphonies* in Philadelphia. Cowell's Fifth was played in Washington. Honegger's work is the portrait of a city, how it looks, how it feels, what it sounds like. Rosenthal's is not a formal symphony at all (hence the plural of the title) but a series of picture postcards, extraordinarily vivid in color, of scenes from the Nativity story. Antheil's piece, on the other hand, is about other symphonies in the same way that Stravinsky's and Hindemith's symphonies are. It is chiefly about Beethoven's Eighth and Prokofiev's *Classical*, I should say. And although it is a well written, vigorous, and thoroughly viable work, it represents an observance of some kind, the ceremony of writing a symphony, perhaps, more than a direct statement about anything beyond its references to the history

Strictly of This Century 109

of symphonic expression. The same applies to William Schuman's and to Harris's symphonies and to Piston's and to Copland's Third, all heard or reheard here in recent seasons. Also to both of Stravinsky's late works in that form and to both of Hindemith's, though the second of these latter has a mood title, *Symphonia Serena*. If it does not quite apply to Milhaud's Second and Third, that is because Milhaud has succeeded, in this listener's judgment, in filling the form with content, not with oratory or with theater but with a deeply personal expression of private feeling, just as Schubert and Mendelssohn and Schumann did a century and more ago.

Cowell's Fifth I have not heard, but the composer's notes make it clear that it embodies researches in both form and expression. It aims at an international communication based not on the cross-reference methods of neoclassicism nor yet on the twelve-tone canonic technique but on the universal applicability of primitive and folklore patterns. This aesthetic is not very different from that of Bartók, though the dominant localism is Celtic-American rather than Balkan. The work's achievement I cannot judge, but certainly its aim is to move us all out of the dead end that the neoclassic symphony appears more and more to be.

The neoclassic symphony is the least successful of all contemporary musical forms, judged by any standard. The picture or landscape symphony is thoroughly successful, but it is not a contemporary form. It is just Mendelssohn's *Scottish* and Debussy's *La Mer*. What the modern world needs is symphonies of private and personal lyricism couched in the language of the modern world. Unfortunately the spiritual resources of the modern world are low for that. The depths of fresh and intense personal feeling that made possible the symphony from Mozart through Schumann are not available anywhere in music today. They exist among Central and East European Jews; but the Jews are using that energy to build a republic, not for supplying repertory to Western concerts. All the new symphonies I have mentioned are good works; but not one, saving possibly the Cowell Fifth, which I do not know, and the Millhaud Second and Third, which have a personal life in them comparable to that of Milhaud's best music of an impersonal character, shows a clear way out of the impasse. Personal lyricism, I am sure, is the ideal way; but in an age characterized by low resources of personal lyricism, depending on them is like making up one's budget to include income that there is no reason whatever for counting on. There might be some chance of an improved result from switching roles, from encouraging the French to write introspectively and the others picturesquely. But Elsa Barraine's Second Symphony, which is French abstractionism, might as well be by a pupil of César Franck. And few of the Americans have anything like the orchestral mastery that it takes to depict the visual. That, of course, they could learn from Manuel Rosenthal.

February 20, 1949

English Landscape

PHILHARMONIC-SYMPHONY ORCHESTRA, LEOPOLD STOKOWSKI, conductor, concert last night in Carnegie Hall. Soloist, BYRON JANIS, pianist.

In the Mountain Country	MOERAN
(First American performance)	
SYMPHONY No. 6	VAUGHAN WILLIAMS
(First New York performance)	
PIANO CONCERTO IN F MAJOR	GERSHWIN
HUNGARIAN RHAPSODY No. 2	LISZT

Ralph Vaughan Williams's Sixth Symphony, composed last year at the age of seventy-five, was the star novelty on last night's Philharmonic program. Whether Leopold Stokowski conducted it with understanding I cannot say, since I had not heard the work before nor seen a score. But it sounded mighty beautiful to me.

Like the rest of this composer's music, it is at once personal and objective, an expression of private feelings and a depiction of English landscape. A neighbor who knows Mr. Williams and his music well tells me the reflective subject matter is war and peace. Also that a good deal of the thematic material and orchestral color of the first movement is quoted or paraphrased from the same composer's ballet *Job*. There is some jigging on the village green, too, an old custom in Mr. Williams's music. Never mind. The piece has power and depth and a very personal, very English beauty. It resembles more the English Romantic poets than it does English art work of our century, though its texture and idiom are modern—modern and medieval, rather. A lovely piece and one I should like to have heard right over again.

In the Mountain Country, a "symphonic impression" by Ernest Moeran, is a youthful work, some twenty-five years old, by a British composer now turned fifty. Pleasantly sweeping but not strikingly original, the material of this is developed in sequence patterns that weaken its impact as a landscape piece. I doubt that it is his most characteristic work, but its color and tunes are not ugly.

George Gershwin's Concerto in F is not an ugly piece, either; but it is a pretty empty one. Even treated to so loud and so irregularly metered a reading as was given it last night by Byron Janis and Mr. Stokowski, it failed to fill with afflatus, though the last movement did move along. All the sweet rapture and ease of the Gershwin style got lost, of course; but virtuosity of another kind came through. That kind, Mr. Janis's kind, is hard and bell-like, clear, dark, steely-fingered. This twenty-year-old boy from Pittsburgh is a whopping piano player both by technique and by temperament. What his musical nature is like one could not tell from one concerto, and that a minor one.

The final novelty of the evening was Liszt's Second Rhapsody, conducted by Mr. Stokowski in the old barnstorming manner one thought he had long since out-grown. It would have been more effective if the orchestra had followed him better. The rendering came off higglety-pigglety, but this reviewer cannot reproach him for having spent his rehearsal time on the Vaughan Williams symphony instead. That was worth pains taken.

January 28, 1949

A String Octet and a Temple Service

The San Francisco bay region's summer music season differs notably from that of most other urban centers in the high seriousness of the programs offered. Not led by climatic intensities to center itself about outdoor circumstances and the intellectually easy-to-take, its repertory regularly includes material that would do honor to any community at any time. Among the new works presented this year, two by Darius Milhaud have had a striking effect on listeners. Unusually impressive both by weight and by volume, their presentation, as well as their composition, represents musical achievement of a high order. It was your correspondent's privilege recently both to hear and to examine the French master's String Octet and his Sacred Service for the Jewish Liturgy.

Milhaud's String Octet is really two String Quartets, numbered in this composer's production Fourteenth and Fifteenth. Intended to be played both separately and together, they were recently so presented in first performance by the Budapest and Paganini Quartets at the University of California in Berkeley. Your correspondent was not present on that occasion; but he listened later, score in hand, to a tape recording of the execution. He also heard the two Quartets played, both separately and simultaneously, by students of Roman Totenberg at the Music Academy of the West in Carpinteria. Their sound, let it be said right off, is an uncommonly tonic musical experience.

Any composer's main problem in writing such a double-barreled work is to differentiate the musical expression of the separate units, to make of them two communications which, when combined, offer a third. The degree to which Milhaud has solved this problem your correspondent would not like to be hasty about estimating. The mere hearing of the double piece, the following of it in sound, is so complex an exercise that judgments of an aesthetic nature must wait upon really learning the piece. Nevertheless, it is clear already that the degree of successful meaning-projection is high.

Quartet No. 14 is a more straightforward lyrical expression than

No. 15. The latter has, I think, poetry of a deeper meditation. Both are composed, as is Milhaud's custom, with the freest use of double harmonies. Even heard alone, they sound pretty dissonant. Heard together, they make a bumping and a jostling that is full of vigor but not at all easy to analyze with the ear. Double harmonies become triple and quadruple to produce a kind of sound that might easily, in the hands of a less skilled polytonalist, have turned into a colorless or muddy gray. It is unquestionably a technical achievement on Milhaud's part to have kept so complex a texture full of light and brightness to the ear.

The first movement of Quartet No. 14 is flowing in character, moderate in animation. That of No. 15, though the tempo of execution is necessarily the same as that of the other, is a light and lively scherzo. In simultaneous performance, the first of these movements tends, I think, to dominate the expression, the second to make commentary on it. The harmony of the two pieces is not always, measure by measure, the same harmony. Consequently, when played as an octet, their sound is fresh.

The two middle movements are even more different. That of No. 14 is a sort of lullaby, that of No. 15 a mystical landscape or pastoral that hardly progresses at all, so intense is its inner dream life. Technically, No. 15 is a four-part reversible canon that after completion turns round on itself and proceeds crabwise back to its beginning. During this latter operation No. 14 performs a thoroughly developed fugue. The effect of the whole, surprisingly, is one of intense luminosity. I am inclined to consider this movement, in all of its forms, the most striking of the three.

The last movement is a jolly rondo in both Quartets; and though no thematic material is ever passed from one to the other, the expressive content in the two is roughly similar. Hearing them together offers a new experience chiefly from the huge fun involved in the way the eight parts elbow one another around. The whole Octet, indeed, is fun to listen to, fun to follow in score, fun to practice swimming around in. Its ultimate value to repertory I have no prescience about, but it seems clear even now that here is a unique composition by a master and that its gustation can offer to music lovers a kind of auditory delight not at all common these days.

Milhaud's Sacred Service, also a double-barreled work, though not one involving superposition, consists of settings for cantor, chorus, and orchestra of both the Friday Evening and the Sabbath Morning Services from the Jewish liturgy. About half the musical matter is common to the two, the rest separately composed. No melodies of traditional origin are employed (save for one briefly), and no evocation of Near East orientalism is allowed to sentimental-ize or to localize a musical conception of universal applicability. The style, though personal to Milhaud, is easily comprehensible anywhere. The service is occasionally bitonal in harmony, often a flowing counterpoint of two or three parts freely juxtaposed, now and then noisily evocative of jostling crowds and alleluias. But for all its occasional brilliance, the service is marked throughout by a tone of intimacy wholly appropriate to the Jewish temple and deeply touching. Its grandeur and its plainness impressed this listener as being somehow related in spirit to those of Purcell and his Eliza-bethan forebears in their settings of Anglican worship forms.

As performed in Berkeley, the composer conducting, or in San Francisco's Temple Emanu-El to organ accompaniment, under the direction of Professor Edward Lawton, with members of the Uni-versity Chorus, the service seemed to this listener a profoundly rev-erent offering both to music and to religion. Not in many a moon has he encountered liturgical music so convincing, so natural, so humane in its utterance. May New York not long delay knowing it!

September 18, 1949

The New Germany and the New Italy

LEAGUE OF COMPOSERS, concert of new European works performed for the first time in the United States last night in Times Hall.

CONCERTO BREVE (1947)   GUIDO TURCHI
    La Salle String Quartet: Walter Levin and Henry Meyer, violinists; Max
    Felde, violist; Jackson Wiley, cellist
SEX CARMINA ALCAEI (1945)   LUIGI DALLAPICCOLA
    Patricia Neway, soprano, and instrumental ensemble; Reginald Stewart, con-
    ductor
Romeo and Juliet (1943)   BORIS BLACHER
    Romeo, Robert Harmon, tenor; Juliet, Eileen Schauler, soprano; Lady Capu-
    let, Cleo Fry, contralto; Capulet, Stanley Kines, bass; chorus and instrumental
    ensemble, Reginald Stewart, conductor

New musical styles from Italy and Germany were the subject of last night's League of Composers concert in Times Hall. A string quartet by Guido Turchi, a set of six monodies with instrumental accompaniment by Luigi Dallapiccola, and a radio opera by Boris Blacher were the examples exposed. The La Salle String Quartet, divers excellent musicians and choral singers from the Juilliard School, and certain admirable vocalists listed above were the executant artists. Reginald Stewart conducted to perfection the works by Dallapiccola and Blacher. Real novelties handsomely performed had brought out a full house of musical personalities.

Blacher's *Romeo and Juliet*, the freshest among the novelties, the most different from standard modern models, is a radio opera based on a cutting of Shakespeare's tragedy in Schlegel's German translation. It was given last night in an adaptation, made partly by the composer, to the original English verses. These fit their musical setting surprisingly well.

The choral and solo parts are everywhere in this opera the point of attention. These are musically most expressive and always rhythmically animated. The instrumental accompaniment is expressive, too, though sparse. With sagacity and skill, Mr. Blacher has reduced this to a skeleton that is functionally no less complete for its extreme

116

thinness. Everything contributes toward throwing the text into high relief. The result is moving and genuinely distinguished.

Blacher represents the new Germany in music. He turns his back on harmonic and contrapuntal complexity and on the romantic afflatus in expression, on all heaviness, obscurity, and introversion of sentiment. He cultivates the elements that have long been absent from German composition, namely, rhythmic life, instrumental wit, harmonic and contrapuntal succinctness, naturalistic declamation. With the simplest of means, he makes a straightforward and meaningful communication.

His influences are chiefly Satie, Kurt Weill, and Stravinsky, though he has neither the commercial folksiness of Weill nor the intellectual ambitions of Stravinsky. The sophisticated plainness of his music is close to that of Satie, though his does not shine with the French master's pure white light. It is invigorating like milk and apples, clean, sensible, healthy, and just what German music needs after a century of overeating.

Whether the twelve-tone style is what Italy needs just now I am not so certain. Perhaps the truth is opposite. Possibly the twelve-tone style can profit from an Italian trip. Certainly Dallapiccola gives to its characteristic broken melodic line a grand lyric quality.

His Sex Carmina Alcaei are a group of poems from the Greek, set for soprano voice and about ten instruments. They are vocally ornate, instrumentally delicate, and warm of expression. They evoke antiquity much as Debussy and Ravel did, by the use of semistatic rhythms, bright instrumental colors, and an impersonal intensity of expression. They are lovely, elegant, sweet, and just the right amount recondite.

Turchi's String Quartet, written two years ago at the age of thirty-one, is the work of an unusually gifted and skillful young man. Dedicated to the memory of Béla Bartók, it imitates the Hungarian master chiefly in its use of spooky sonorities. These are applied with imagination and a light hand. The last movement has rhythmic life in it, too. The whole piece is graceful, sensitive, serious. It will be a pleasure to hear more from this composer.

April 11, 1949

Ragtime Revived

Back in the 1890's and around the turn of the century, ragtime was new, popular, sinful. By 1910 it had lost both its novelty and its sinful quality to jazz, but it was still popular. In 1920 it was out of style; jazz ruled the roost. In the 1930's swing came along and did to jazz what jazz had done two decades earlier to ragtime. Nowadays jazz, swing, and ragtime are all old-fashioned; bebop has the new and shocking quality. The earlier styles are just chamber music.

It is not the privilege of this observer to choose among them; but it has amused him to notice that the scholarly enthusiasts, the aesthetic polemicists, and the record collectors who admire American popular music intensely behave toward it very much as the long-hairs do toward European classical music. Their respect is in proportion to its age in the modern world. Victorian popular music is obviously prehistoric, just as the music written before Bach is to the ear of an average classical music lover. In spite of research and revivals, Bach remains the beginning for us of everything that is really ours. And just so, ragtime is basic American to all who hold dear the national vernacular of our time. Out of that has come all the rest, even the bebop that is so despised, as swing was before it, by the defenders of tradition.

It was the pleasure of your reporter on Saturday a week ago to hear devoted to ragtime, at the Carl Fischer Auditorium on West Fifty-seventh Street, a whole concert, "the first ever given in New York history," according to Mr. Rudi Blesh, who introduced it. The artists were impeccable; the program was distinguished. A trio known as The Ragpickers consisted on this occasion of Tony Parenti, clarinetist, Ralph Sutton, pianist, and Tony Spargo, drummer. (The latter, a veteran of the Original Dixieland Jazz Band, used to be known as Toni Sbarbaro.) All three are technical masters and musicians of refined style, as becomes the exponents of a classical repertory. If any of them seemed to this listener more remarkable than the others, it was the pianist. Perhaps we are more used to fine clarinet and

118

drum playing than to pianism of Mr. Sutton's solid standards. In any case, I found the latter most satisfying. The program was as follows:

I

Maple Leaf Rag	SCOTT JOPLIN
That Eccentric Rag	J. RUSSEL ROBINSON
Clarinet Marmalade	SHIELDS-SBARBARO
Sensation	EDDIE EDWARDS

II

Hysterics	BRESE-KLICKMAN
Grace and Beauty	JAMES SCOTT
Praline	TONY PARENTI
Swipesy Cake Walk	JOPLIN-MARSHALL
Hiawatha	NEIL MORET
Sunflower Slow Drag	JOPLIN-HAYDEN

III

Whitewash Man	JEAN SCHWARTZ
Twelfth Street Rag	BOWMAN
Dill Pickles	CHARLES L. JOHNSON
St. Louis Blues Fantasy	W. C. HANDY

IV

Cataract Rag	ROBERT HAMPTON
Crawfish Crawl	TONY PARENTI
Nonsense Rag	R. G. BRADY
Red Head Rag	IRENE FRANKLIN-GREEN
The Lily Rag	CHARLES THOMPSON
The Entertainers Rag	JAY ROBERTS

Group III consisted of piano solos. The rest was ensemble playing, enlivened by frequent solos. Historic pieces like *Hiawatha* and the *Maple Leaf Rag, Dill Pickles,* the *Twelfth Street Rag,* and many another ditty famed in story gave it a remembrance-of-things-past appeal. *The St. Louis Blues,* that Fifth Symphony of the jazz world, made it legal.

Your announcer has no intention of criticizing the concert in detail. He is not one of ragtime's detail men. He found the whole thing thoroughly distinguished and delightful. He also enjoyed the audience, which consisted largely of quiet, well-behaved young people. It was no house of transported "alligators" or jittering "cats" from the swing days and still less of holy-rolling bebopers. It was like college boys and girls listening to Mozart. They were wide awake, respectful, thoroughly interested but not taking part in the show. I wish you all could have shared, as I did, their lively attention. I wish, too, that a great many more concerts of this kind were given in New York. This one's excellence was comparable to that of the best offered here in "standard" music.

April 24, 1949

Hollywood's Best

Aaron Copland's musical accompaniments to a film called *The Red Pony* (by Milestone, out of Steinbeck) are the most elegant, in my opinion, yet composed and executed under "industry conditions," as Hollywood nowadays calls itself. Other films shown this winter have had ambitious scoring or talented sonorous detail, but those this writer has seen have not offered any consistently distinguished music. Mr. Copland himself, Hollywood's most accomplished composer, has not in his earlier films—*Of Mice and Men, The North Star,* and *Our Town*—produced for cinematic drama a musical background so neatly cut and fitted.

It is the perfection of the musical tailoring in this picture that has made clear to me in a way I had not understood before just where the artistic error lies in the industry's whole manner of treating musical backgrounds. Hollywood has often engaged high-class composers, but Hollywood has also been notoriously unable to use these in any high-class way. European films have made better use of the big musical talents than we have. Honegger, Auric, Milhaud, and Sauguet in France, William Walton in England, Kurt Weill in Germany, Prokofiev and Shostakovitch in Soviet Russia have all made film music that was more than a worthy contribution to film drama. Here privately produced or government-produced documentaries have occasionally made film and music history, but our industry-produced fiction films have not included in their whole lifetime five musico-dramatic productions worthy to rank beside the fifty or more European films that as musico-dramatic compositions merit the name "work of art."

It is not talent or skill that is lacking here. It is not intelligence, either, or general enlightenment on the part of directors and producers. The trouble goes deep and has, I think, to do with our distribution rather than with our production system. But first let me talk a bit about *The Red Pony*.

The film itself, as a visual narrative, is far from perfect. It is diffuse; it tries to tell more stories than it can integrate with the main one or bring to a conclusion. Also, it has too many stars in it. It is about a boy and a pony, both admirably played. What the child star and the animal need is acting support, not glamour support. What they get, however, is not acting support at all but the glamour competition of Robert Mitchum and Myrna Loy. As a result, the composer has been obliged to hold the show together with music. There are some sixty minutes of this; and Mr. Copland has made it all interesting, various, expressive. If he has not made it all equally pointed, that is not his fault. He has met beautifully and effectively all the possible kinds of musical demand but one. That one is the weak spot in all American fiction films. It is a result of our particular treatment of the female star.

Wherever Copland has provided landscape music, action music, or a general atmosphere of drama he has worked impeccably. Here his music sets a scene, illustrates action, advances the story. Wherever he has essayed to interpret the personal and private feelings of Miss Loy, he has obscured the décor, stopped the action, killed the story, exactly as Miss Loy herself has done at those moments. His music at such times goes static and introspective, becomes, for dramatic purposes, futile. In a landscape picture, which this is, interpreting emotion directly in the music destroys the pastoral unity of tone. Miss Loy's sadness about her marital maladjustment might have been touching against a kind of music that suggested the soil, the land, the farm, the country life—all those attachments which, not shared by her husband, are the causes of her sadness. But the sadness itself, when blown up to concert size and deprived of specific musical allusion, loses point. The composer here may have helped to build up the glamour of the actress; but he has, by doing so, allowed the author's narrative to collapse.

American films have occasionally omitted all such fake *Tristan und Isolde* music, using simply dialogue or sound effects to support the stars' close-ups. It is much easier, moreover, to handle musically a male star in emotional crisis than a female one, since our mythology allows character and even picturesqueness to the hero. Our heroines, on the other hand, are supposed to be nymphs— all grooming, all loveliness, all abstract desirability, though capable of an intense despair when crossed in love. It is not easy to make a successful picture about one of these goddesses unless the contributing elements—music, costumes, furniture, housing, male adoration, effects of weather, and triumphs of technology—are made to contribute to the myth. Our industry, our whole design, manufacture, and distribution of fiction films, is the commerce of this goddess's image. She is what Hollywood makes and sells. It is easy for a classically trained composer, one for whom art means reality, to enhance the reality of scenic backgrounds, to animate passages of action, to emphasize dramatic values, to give shape and pacing to any narrative's progress. But it is quite impossible for him to be a salesman of soul states in which he does not believe.

No composer working in Hollywood, not even the great Copland himself, has ever made me believe that he believed in the reality of our female stars' emotions. That is the spot where American films go phony, where they fail of truth to life. In so far as this spot is a box-office necessity (and with million-dollar budgets it may well be a necessity), it is impossible for the film industry to make a musico-dramatic work of art. The film, as Europe has proved, is an art form capable of using to advantage the collaboration of the best composers. The film as produced by the American industry has never been able to show any composer at his best. *The Red Pony*, in spite of its mediocrity as a film drama, comes nearer to doing this than other American fiction films I have seen. It is the nearness of its miss, indeed, that has made me realize where the fault in our Hollywood musical credo lies. It lies in the simple truth that it is not possible to write real music about an unreal emotion. An actress can communicate an unreal emotion, because tears, any tears, are contagious. But no composer can transform a feeling into beauty unless he knows in his heart that that feeling is the inevitable response of a sane human being to unalterable events.

April 10, 1949

V. IN MEMORY OF...

Claude Debussy

Thirty years ago last Friday, on March 26, 1918, Claude Debussy died in his fifty-sixth year. Though his three decades of artistic productivity lie on both sides of the century-mark, just as Beethoven's did a hundred years earlier, musically he is as clearly a founding father of the twentieth century as Beethoven was of the nineteenth. The history of music in our time, like any other history, is fully to be reviewed only in the light of all its origins and all its roots. Nevertheless, modern music, the full flower of it, the achievement rather than the hope, stems from Debussy. Everybody who wrote before him is just an ancestor and belongs to another time. Debussy belongs to ours.

124

It is doubtful, indeed, whether Western music has made any notable progress at all since his death. Neoclassicism, the evoking of ancient styles in general and of the early eighteenth-century styles in particular, he invented. Even atonality, the consistent employment of contradictory chromatics, is present in his later works, notably in the ballet *Jeux*. No succeeding composer has augmented his dissonant intensity, though some have made a louder noise. Stravinsky's early picturesque works and his later formalistic ones are no more radical in either sound or structure than Debussy's landscape pieces and his sonatas. Schönberg's twelve-tone row, though Debussy never knew it, is merely a systematization, a rule of thumb to make atonal writing easy. Expressively it has added nothing to the gamut of sensibility that Debussy created and Schönberg adopted. If, as Busoni believed, one could reconstruct the whole German classic and Romantic repertory out of Sebastian Bach alone, certainly modern music, all of it, could be rebuilt from the works of Debussy.

What music has lost since Debussy's death is sensitivity of expression and expressivity of instrumentation. Our feelings are more brutal and our statements about them less precise. Similarly, our language of chord dispositions and musical sounds is less competent, less richly evocative than his. We have all gone in for broader, cruder effects. We have had to, because his way of writing was at the end of his life almost unbearably delicate. Refinement could be pushed no further, though Anton Webern tried and succeeded at least in not falling far short of Debussy's mark. But the others could not face going on in that way. Sensibly they turned to easier paths. The fact remains, nevertheless, that Debussy's work is more radical than theirs and, in the ways both of expression and of the use of musical materials to this end, more powerful.

Curiously enough, Debussy's employment of orchestral sound, though commonly described as "colorful," was not so envisaged by him. Variety of coloration is certainly present, and knowingly, in his piano writing. Like that of Schumann and that of Mozart, it is full of the imitation of both orchestral and naturalistic sound-effects. But he avowed the aim of *Fêtes*, for instance, to be monochromatic, "a musical equivalent of the *grisaille*," which is a watercolor or ink brush-drawing done entirely in grays. The secret here is that Debussy did not, in this piece or in any other, ever, save for purposes of avoiding them, seriously respect the gamut of orchestral weights. He used the orchestral palette as the Impressionist painters used theirs, not for the accenting of particular passages but for the creation of a general luminosity. And the surface tension of his scores in performance is no less equalized than that of a Renoir, a Pissarro, a Monet canvas. Something like this must have been what he meant by comparing them to a *grisaille*.

Debussy's instrumentation, though it is an advance over Berlioz, is derived from the latter's practice, from the use of sound as a purely acoustical phenomenon. He depersonalizes all instruments. His piano writing, too, though an advance over Chopin's, is derived from that of the Great One. It is not designed, like that of Liszt, for ease of execution but all for delighting the ear and for making music mean things. His melody is Massenet purified, plainsong, and memories of popular song. His counterpoint, though rarefied almost to the point of non-existence, is straight out of Mozart by way of the Paris Conservatory. Every line communicates. Even his harmony, for all its imaginative quality and its freedom, is made up out of Satie plus a taste for the archaic. Maybe there is just a touch of Moussorgsky, too. But his profound originality lies in his concept of formal structure. Where he got it I do not know. It may come out of Impressionist painting or Symbolist poetry. Certainly there is small precedent for it in music. It remains, nevertheless, his most radical gift to the art.

This formal pattern is a mosaic texture made up of tiny bits and pieces all fitted in together so tightly that they create a continuity. The structural lines of the composition are not harmonic, not in the bass, but rhythmic and melodic. Debussy freed harmony from its rhetorical function, released it wholly to expression. He gave everything to expression, even structure. He did not sculpt in music or build architectural monuments. He only painted. And no two of his canvases are alike. They are all different and all intensely communicative. The range of their effective expression is the largest our century has known, the largest that music has known since Mozart. Piano music, the song, the violin sonata, the cello, chamber music, the opera, the oratorio, the orchestral concert piece all receive from his hand a new liberty, say things and mean things they had never said or tried to mean before. His power over all the musical usages and occasions comes from his complete disrespect for the musical forms and from his ability to replace these by a genuinely satisfactory free continuity.

That France, classically the land of freedom, should have produced a model of musical freedom is only natural. All the same, Debussy, even for France, is something of a miracle. No composer ever wrote with such absence of cliché, detailed or formal. And few have achieved such precision, such intensity, such wide range of expression. His music is not only an ultimate, for our century, of sheer beauty. It is a lesson to us all in how to make use of our liberty.

Isidore Philipp, the great piano pedagogue, now in his middle eighties, tells of a visit received in Paris from Béla Bartók, then a young man. He offered to introduce the young Hungarian composer to Camille Saint-Saëns, at that time a terrific celebrity. Bartók declined. Philipp then offered him Charles-Marie Widor. Bartók again declined: "Well, if you won't meet Saint-Saëns and Widor, who is there that you would like to know?" "Debussy," said Bartók. "But he is a horrid man," said Philipp. "He hates everybody and will certainly be rude to you. Do you want to be insulted by Debussy?" "Yes," said Bartók.

March 28, 1948

Maurice Ravel

Ten years ago next month, December 28, 1937, Maurice Ravel died. He was not old, only sixty-two. Many people living knew him well. I knew him myself a little. He was cultivated, charming, companionable, neither timid nor bold, in no way difficult. That is why he is not today, nor was he during his lifetime, a misunderstood man or a misunderstood composer. For all its complexity of texture, wealth of invention, and profound technical originality, his work presents fewer difficulties of comprehension than that of any of the other great figures of the modern movement. Satie, Debussy, Schönberg, Webern, Stravinsky all remain, in many facets of their expression, hermetic. Ravel has never been obscure, even to the plain public. His early work produced a shock, but only the shock of complete clarity. Anybody could dislike it or turn his back, still can. Nobody could fail, nobody ever has failed to perceive at first sight what it is all about.

What it is all about is a nonromantic view of life. Not an anti-romantic view, simply a nonromantic one, as if the nineteenth century had never, save for its technical discoveries, existed. All the other modernists were children of Romanticism—worshipful children, like Schönberg, or children in revolt, like Stravinsky, or children torn, like Debussy, between atavism and an imperious passion for independence. Even Satie felt obliged to poke fun at the Romantics from time to time. But for Ravel there was no such temptation, no Romantic problem. When twentieth-century models failed him he had recourse to eighteenth-century ones. And he used these not at all to prove any point against the nineteenth century, but simply because they were the most natural thing in the world for him to be using. Couperin, Rameau, and Haydn were as close to him as Chabrier and Fauré, his immediate masters.

Maurice Ravel was not interested in posing as a prophet, as a poet, or as a writer of editorials. He was no sybil, no saint, no oracle nor sacred pythoness. He was simply a skilled workman who enjoyed his work. In religion a skeptic, in love a bachelor, in social life a semirecluse, a suburbanite, he was not in any of these aspects a disappointed man. He was jolly, generous, a wit, a devoted friend, and as much of a *viveur* as his none too solid health and his temperate tastes permitted. His was an adult mind and a good mind, tender, ironic, cultivated, sharply observant. He was kind but not foolish, humane but not sentimental, easygoing but neither self-indulgent nor lazy. There was acid in him but no bile; and he used his acid as a workman does, for etching.

He considered art, and said so, to be, at its best, artifice, and the artist an artisan. For all the clarity that his music embodies, its crystalline lucidity in every phrase, it probably expresses less of personal sentiment than any of the other major music of our century. He worked in the free Impressionistic style, in the straight dance forms, in the classic molds of chamber music, and for the lyric stage. His masterpiece is a ballet. Always he worked objectively, with the modesty of an architect or a jeweler, but with the assurance of a good architect or a good jeweler. He was equally master of the miniature and of the grander lay-outs. At no necessary point does his expression lack either subtlety or magnitude. It lacks nothing, as a matter of fact, except those qualities that are equally lacking, for instance, in La Fontaine and in Montaigne, namely, animal warmth, mysticism, and the darker aspects of spirituality.

Ravel was a classical composer, because his music presents a straightforward view of life in clear and durable form. The straightforwardness and the clarity are, I think, obvious. The durability will be no less so if you consider the hard usage that *La Valse*, *Daphnis et Chloë* (at least the Second Suite from it), the Bolero, the *Pavane for a Dead Princess*, the Piano Sonatina, and *Scarbo*, a pianists' war horse, have been put through already. I call them durable because they stand up under usage. And they stand up under usage because they are well made. They are well made because they are clearly conceived and executed by an objective and responsible hand. The hand is objective and responsible in the way that it is because it is a French hand, one that inherits the oldest unbroken tradition in Europe of objective and responsible artisanry.

Ravel's music represents, even more than does that of Debussy, who was more deeply touched than he by both the Slavic and the Germanic impulses toward a spiritualization of the emotional life, the classic ideal that is every Frenchman's dream and every foreigner's dream of France. It is the dream of an equilibrium in which sentiment, sensuality, and the intelligence are united at their highest intensity through the operations of a moral quality. That moral quality, in Ravel's case, and indeed in the case of any first-class artist, is loyalty, a loyalty to classic standards of workmanship, though such loyalty obliges its holder to no observance whatsoever of classical methods. It is an assumption of the twin privileges, freedom and responsibility. The success that Ravel's music has known round the world is based, I am convinced, on its moral integrity. It has charm, wit, and no little malice. It also has a sweetness and a plain humanity about it that are deeply touching. Add to these qualities the honesty of precise workmanship; and you have a product, an artifact, as Bernard Berenson would call it, that is irresistible.

France has for centuries produced this kind of art work and, for all the trials of the flesh and of the spirit that she is suffering just now, is continuing to produce it. Rosenthal, Sauguet, Poulenc, Jolivet, Barraud, Rivier, and the dodecaphonic young, these and dozens more have vowed their lives to sincerity of expression and to high standards of workmanship. The music of Milhaud and Messiaen has even grander aspirations. But all French composers, whether they care to admit it or not, are in debt to Ravel. It was he, not Gounod nor Bizet nor Saint-Saëns nor Massenet, nor yet César Franck nor Debussy, who gave to France its contemporary model of the composer. That model is the man of simple life who is at once an intellectual by his tastes and an artisan by his training and by his practice. He is not a bourgeois nor a white-collar proletarian nor a columnist nor a priest nor a publicized celebrity nor a jobholder nor a political propagandist—but simply and plainly, proudly and responsibly, a skilled workman. Long may the model survive!

November 30, 1947

Kurt Weill

Kurt Weill, who died last Monday at the age of fifty, was a composer who will be missed. Nothing he touched came out banal. Everything he wrote became in one way or another historic. He was probably the most original single workman in the whole musical theater, internationally considered, during the last quarter century.

His originality consisted in an ability to handle all the forms of the musical theater with freedom, to make them expressive, to build structures with them that serve a story and sustain a play. He was not a natural melodist like Richard Rodgers or George Gershwin, though he turned out some memorable tunes. Nor was he a master of thematic development, though he could hold a long scene together impeccably. He was an architect, a master of musico-dramatic design, whose structures, built for function and solidity, constitute a repertory of models that have not only served well their original purpose but also had wide influence as examples of procedure.

Weill came to the light musical theater, for which most of his American works were conceived, from a classical training (he was the pupil of Humperdinck and of Busoni) and long experience of the artistic, the experimental theater. His literary collaborators were consistently writers of distinction. Georg Kaiser, Ivan Goll, Berthold Brecht, Arnold Sundgaard, and Maxwell Anderson were among them. Brecht was the librettist of the epoch-marking works of his German period—*Der Jasager, Der Dreigroschenoper* and *Aufstieg und Fall der Stadt Mahagonny.* Also of a ballet with words, composed in Paris, *Les Sept Péchés Capitaux,* played in England as *Anna-Anna.*

These works have transformed the German opera. Their simplicity of style and flexibility of form have given, indeed, to present-day Germany its only progressive movement in music. Without them the work of Boris Blacher and Hans Orff would be inconceivable. Without their example also we would not have had in America Marc Blitzstein's powerful *The Cradle Will Rock* and *No for an Answer.* Whether Weill's American works will carry as far as his German ones I cannot say. They lack the mordant and touching humanity of Brecht's poetry. They also lack a certain acidity in the musical characterization that gave cutting edge to Weill's musical style when he worked in the German language.

Nevertheless, they are important to history. His last musical play, *Lost in the Stars,* for all that it lacks the melodic appeal of

Mahagonny and even of *Lady in the Dark,* is a masterpiece of musical application to dramatic narrative; and its score, composed for twelve players, is Weill's finest work of orchestral craft. His so-called "folk-opera," *Down in the Valley,* is not without strength either. Easy to perform and dramatically perfect, it speaks an American musical dialect that Americans can accept. Its artfulness is so concealed that the whole comes off as naturally as a song by Stephen Foster, though it lasts a good half hour.

Weill was the last of our local light theater musicians to orchestrate his own scores and the last to have full mastery of composition. He could make music move in and out of a play with no effect of shock. He could write a ballet, a song, a complex finale with equal ease. (A successful Broadway composer once asked me, "What is a finale?") These skills may turn up again in our light theater, but for the present they are gone. Or they may be replaced by the ability of Menotti, Blitzstein, and other classically trained composers to hold public attention through constructed tragic music dramas. Just at present the American musical theater is rising in power. But its lighter wing has lost in Kurt Weill a workman who might have bridged for us the gap, as he did in Germany, between grand opera and the *singspiel.* The loss to music and to the theater is real. Both will go on, and so will Weill's influence. But his output of new models—and every new work was a new model, a new shape, a new solution of dramatic problems—will not continue. Music has lost a creative mind and a master's hand.

April 9, 1950

Béla Bartók

Béla Bartók's music, always respected by musicians, seems now, some three years after his death, to be coming into its reward of

132

love. Not only is the number of musicians who are attached to it increasing; laymen are beginning to bear it affection. Every orchestra plays a Bartók piece now once a year, and his string quartets appear regularly on the chamber music programs. The Juilliard String Quartet played three of these last month, will complete the cycle of six at Times Hall on Monday evening, the 28th of this month.

This examiner has never been deeply impressed with the technical originality of Bartók. His major virtues, in my view, lie in the expressive domain. He was a master, of course. He had a good ear and abundant fancy. He knew the technical innovations of our century, used most of them, invented innumerable small adaptations or variants of them. But there is very little of textural ingenuity in his music that could not have been derived by any active musical mind from the works of Debussy and Stravinsky. Exactly such a mind, that of Manuel de Falla, did derive a comparable rhetoric from those sources, employing Spanish local color as Bartók did Hungarian and achieving a musical result not essentially different, a nationalistically oriented Impressionism admirably suited to evoking the dance.

Bartók, however, though he began as a picturesque composer, had another string to his harp. He wrote chamber music of a reflective character. Impressionism was paralleled in his practice not by neoclassic constructions, as was the practice of Western composers (even de Falla, in his harpsichord concerto, essayed the formal), but by Expressionism, by an outpouring of private feelings that is related as an aesthetic method both to the loose formal observances of nineteenth-century Central European chamber music and to that extreme subjectivity of expression that is characteristic of Arnold Schönberg's early works.

The formal preoccupations of Western neoclassicism do not lend themselves easily to emotional effusion, and neither do the techniques of picturesque sound. Emotional outpourings work best with loose structures and a gray palette. So Bartók kept his continuity loose, abbreviating it more and more into a semblance of tight form, and neutralized his color. At heart, however, he loved bright colors; and in his concertos he continued to employ them. In his later quartets he replaced surface color with emotional vividness. And if this last is less lurid and private than it is in Schönberg's chamber works, it is no less tonic.

Hans Heinsheimer, visiting a Boston performance of Bartók's Concerto for Orchestra, has recounted how at the end of the piece a neighbor turned to her husband and said, "Conditions must be terrible in Europe." She was right, of course. They were, especially in Central Europe, where Bartók lived. And she was right in sensing their relation to the expressive content of Bartók's music. It is here, I think, that his nobility of soul is most impressive. The despair in his quartets is no personal maladjustment. It is a realistic facing, through the medium of pure feeling, of the human condition, the state of man as a moral animal, as this was perceptible to a musician of high moral sensibilities living in Hungary.

No other musician of our century has faced its horrors quite so frankly. The quartets of Bartók have a sincerity, indeed, and a natural elevation that are well-nigh unique in the history of music. I thing it is this lofty quality, their intense purity of feeling that gives them warmth and that makes their often rude and certainly deliberate discordance of sound acceptable to so many music lovers of otherwise conservative tastes. Nobody, as we know, ever minds expressive discord. The "modern music" war was a contest over the right to enjoy discord for its own sake, for its spicy tang and for the joy it used to give by upsetting applecarts. Bartók himself, as a young man, was a spice lover but not at all an upsetter. He was a consolidator of advance rather than a pioneer. As a mature composer he came to lose his taste for paprika but not for humanity. His music approached more and more a state of systematic discord, rendered more and more truly and convincingly the state of European man in his time. His six string quartets are the cream of Bartók's repertory, the essence of his deepest thought and feeling, his most powerful and humane communication. They are also, in a century that has produced richly in that medium, a handful of chamber music nuggets that are pure gold by any standards.

March 20, 1949

VI. FROM OUT OF TOWN

The Berkshire Music Center

The Festival Concerts of the Berkshire Music Center at Tanglewood, near Lenox, Massachusetts, long nationally famous, are attended by a large and demonstrative audience. The scholastic activities of the center, though they serve a much smaller number of persons, are internationally held in high repute; and entry either to the faculty or to the student body of these is considered an honor among musicians of Europe and South America, as well as among those of this continent. Indeed, the school shows its director, Serge Koussevitzky, in a most becoming new role, that of pedagogue. As interpreter, publisher, and patron of living composers, he has a half-cen-

135

tury of loyal service behind him. Last Tuesday his seventy-fifth birthday found him in a fourth position, that of educator, and with nearly a decade of achievement to his credit in that capacity.

The Berkshire Music Center is not, as many of its good neighbors imagine, mainly a concert-giving organization. As such it would be of only local interest. Its international prestige comes from the fact that it is a top-standard professional music school. The Festival concerts, in this conception of Tanglewood, are a peripheral activity, an icing on the cake. Artistically, of course, they need no apology. But economically, too, they are of value, since their profits (and they do make profits) go toward the upkeep of the school. Also, the personnel of the orchestra provides a faculty for professional instruction that would be hard to match anywhere in the world. The school is built about the orchestra and depends on the orchestra. It offers to the orchestra, in return, an outlet for the orchestra's individual and collective abilities that tends in this particular time to outrank as a cultural influence even the orchestra's known value as a concert instrument.

The school has five departments—conducting, orchestral playing, musical composition, operatic performance, and choral singing. All lie under the general direction of Dr. Koussevitzky and of his assistant, Aaron Copland, both of whom direct departments and teach classes as well, the former assuming responsibility for the students of conducting and the latter for those of composition. In the conducting department Dr. Koussevitzky is assisted orchestrally by Richard Burgin, Leonard Bernstein, and Eleazar de Carvalho, chorally by Hugh Ross and Christopher Honass. Every Friday there is an orchestral concert of which the conducting is shared between one of these professionals and one of the more advanced conducting students.

The orchestra at these concerts is a group of 110 players, all students in the department of orchestral performance. The faculty of the latter is made up of first-desk players from the Boston Symphony Orchestra and known chamber music specialists. These last, this year, are Gregor Piatigorsky, William Kroll, and the members of

136

the Juilliard Quartet. Students in this department play both in orchestral and in chamber-music groups.

The composition students are shared between Aaron Copland and a distinguished foreign composer. This year Olivier Messiaen is the guest, succeeding Darius Milhaud, Arthur Honneger, and comparable masters. There is both class and private instruction. Every Sunday night there is a concert at which works by the young composers are performed by singers and instrumentalists from the other departments.

Opera is the province of Boris Goldowsky. His students consist of thirty singers (chosen by audition), of forty auditors, and of divers technical aspirants. These learn not only the art of singing in opera but also conducting, stage direction, scenery and costume design, lighting, and all such contributory techniques. There are four students vowed to the rare, special, and deplorably misunderstood art of libretto writing. The opera department has its own theater and its own student orchestra, produces every year whole acts or scenes from standard operas and two rare lyric stage works entire, an old and a new one. This year the complete productions will be Gluck's *Iphigenia in Tauris*, in English, and Benjamin Britten's *Albert Herring*. The former is a classic work seldom heard in the United States. The latter, a comic piece based on de Maupassant's *Le Rosier de Madame Husson*, has never been heard here at all, though it has had considerable success in England.

The fifth department, that of choral singing, formerly the charge of Robert Shaw, is at present in the equally capable hands of Hugh Ross and Christopher Honass. The students sing in three groupings, the largest being that of the Festival Chorus, employed for choral works in the Festival concerts. The others are a Madrigal Chorus, which sings historic works from medieval, Renaissance, and modern times, and a Bach Choir, which gives cantatas and like masterpieces from the period of the Lutheran Baroque. This department has also its own student orchestra.

What with the big Festival concerts, the smaller Bach-Mozart series, the opera productions, the weekly concerts of the No. 1 student orchestra, the chamber-music concerts, choral concerts, composers' concerts, and I don't know what all else, there is constantly available to the students music old and new in executions of the highest quality and in a repertory remarkable for its breadth. Selected students (465 of them at present) from all over the world, a faculty of first-class practicing artists, and a wide-range cultural program of the best music impeccably performed all go to make a pedagogic institution of great value. Though this chiefly serves professional aspirants, the layman also has a place in the scheme through the classes in choral singing, which, by offering real musical exercise, are of value toward raising cultural standards in general.

The weakness in so nearly ideal an institution is the fact that it is merely a summer school. Limited to six weeks' time, any course tends to become just a glimpse. Mr. Copland told your reporter during a recent visit to Tanglewood that he considered the major value of the school to be the stimulation it offers to students and instructors from their brief but intense encounters. Many young professional musicians do, in fact, go back year after year for just that stimulation. It is to be wished that eventually musical schools of comparable standards, working on a full-time schedule, can be formed around other great symphonic foundations. Serge Koussevitzky and the Berkshire Music Center have given us a model of procedure. Tanglewood is what all our musical pedagogy *must* look toward for professional standards and what our symphony orchestras *should* look toward for the fulfilling of their cultural possibilities. Also, I suspect, for solving their budget problems in the second part of this century. Because education is always clearly worth its price, whereas mere concerts, however cultural, may not always be found so.

July 31, 1949

The Delights of Denver

Denver in the summer offers to the visitor more of music and theatrical entertainment than most cities can provide at any time of year. Not to speak of a hospitality that is unique for abundance and charm. There are two stock companies, an excellent symphony orchestra, student plays and operatic productions at the university, and, at nearby Central City, opera of the first class in a setting that is both stylish and of historical interest. The symphony orchestra itself plays both popular-type and intellectual programs. The former are given once a week at Elitch's Gardens, a large amusement park which incloses also a theater, the seat of one of the oldest summer stock companies in America, founded in 1890, at present directed by Norris Houghton. The intellectual programs are presented at Red Rocks Theater, an outdoor auditorium in the mountains, some seventeen miles from the city, a site of the highest natural beauty and architectural distinction.

Saul Caston, formerly first trumpet of the Philadelphia Orchestra and assistant to both Leopold Stokowski and Eugene Ormandy, is musical director of the Denver Symphony Orchestra. In three years, under his leadership, the group has become one of the major orchestras of America, estimated by either artistic or budgetary standards. Your correspondent heard a "pop" concert at Elitch's and a Red Rocks program. Both were marked by fine solo work in the wind sections, by delicacy and precision of string playing and by impeccable musicianship in conducting. The first was led by Mr. Caston himself. The second, largely prepared by Mr. Caston in preliminary rehearsals, was conducted by Igor Stravinsky. No other summer orchestra enjoys, to my knowledge, quite the rehearsal luxury of this one. Mr. Caston has a full rehearsal (three times the preparation of the Boston Pops) for each popular concert and five for each concert at Red Rocks (ten times that of our Lewisohn Stadium programs), a figure approached, though still not equaled, only by the Boston Symphony Orchestra playing in Tanglewood. All this care shows up, of course, in the quality of the execution.

The Red Rocks concert that your correspondent heard was marked by the American debut of the pianist Soulima Stravinsky and by a work unfamiliar, in its present form, to New Yorkers, a Divertimento, or Suite, from Igor Stravinsky's ballet *Le Baiser de la Fée*. The latter was preceded by Igor's Capriccio for Piano and Orchestra, Soulima playing the solo part, by Tchaikovsky's Second Symphony, and by Glinka's *Russlan and Ludmilla* overture. The Divertimento, melodious music no less charming in concert than in theatrical presentation, will probably achieve a merited currency. Its performance at Red Rocks was gravely marred by the presence on the stage throughout its duration of three photographers, employees of a nationally circulated magazine, who walked around and rattled flash bulbs in seeming unawareness that the occasion had any other purpose than providing them with a subject. That the piece could be attended to at all against such visual and even auditory distraction is evidence of its solid qualities and also of Igor Stravinsky's iron-willed power as a conductor. The audience, in gratitude, gave him a long ovation with cries of "More, Igor!" and "Encore, Igor!"

Soulima Stravinsky had previously been acclaimed at length and had played, after the Capriccio, three encores. The demonstration had seemed, to this listener, fully merited, though he would not like to pronounce, from one performance in a concerted work and three short pieces, all heard outdoors, on the full quality of Soulima Stravinsky as a piano virtuoso. That he is a musician of refinement and sound taste was clear from his renderings of a Stravinsky Etude and two works by Scarlatti. That he has a better than average technical equipment was also clear, though transcendent virtuosity was nowhere in evidence. His work throughout was clean and musicianly, his tone and passage work dry, in the best contemporary taste. The most impressive element of the performance was the authoritative, the definitive character of the Capriccio's interpretation. Igor and Soulima Stravinsky understand the piece in the same way, play it as a real duet, with the greatest freedom and firmness. There should be no questioning henceforth of the work's essential character. The way the Stravinskys play it is the way it goes and the way it should, within any artist's temperamental limitations, be made to go.

140

The performances of my own opera *The Mother of Us All* at Denver University, being student work, are not properly a subject for public criticism, though I should like to commend the ingeniousness and imagination of their staging, which was the work of Roi White. Neither shall I go farther in reporting performances of the summer theater troupes than to attest that I enjoyed the one I saw. Let me give what space I have to the big-time theatrical executions, those given at the Central City Opera House. I shall also skip briefly over the architectural and other delights of that locale, a gold mining town of the 1870's with a theater and hotel of noble design and two of the best bars in America. Of the physical advantages let me only remark, because of its determining influence on the brilliance of the opera performances, that the Central City Opera House, seating some 700, has an acoustical liveness, a fullness of resonance without any echo, that is not equaled by more than a half dozen houses of its kind in the world. It is completely advantageous to music, makes everything sound bright and warm.

That the performances were worthy of their enhancement is due to the producer, Frank St. Leger, and to the chief conductor, Emil Cooper. These musicians assembled this year two casts of first-line singers and an excellent orchestra and with the aid of Herbert Graf, stage director, and of Donald Oenslager, designer, produced two operas, which were given on alternate nights for twenty-five performances in July. The season's works were Mozart's *Così fan tutte* and Offenbach's *Contes d'Hoffmann*, both sung in English. For general musical excellence the performances were the equal of any opera performances available anywhere today and far, far better than many produced in more pretentious circumstances. For specific excellence, vocal and histrionic, I should like to mention the work of Jerome Hines as both Coppelius and Miracle in *Hoffmann* and of Graciela Silvain, who sang Olympia in the same opera. This admirable singer, an Argentinian, not yet heard in New York, may well be our first coloratura for the next decade or two. Her voice has brightness and body, and she is obviously both a musician and an artist. Surrounding these exceptional performances were the handsome vocalism of Igor Gorin, who sang Lindorff and Dappertutto, of Philip Kinsman as Schlemil, and of a fine dramatic soprano hitherto unknown to this reviewer, Mariquita Moll, who sang Giulietta. The rest of the cast, which was good, if vocally less striking, contained many famous and about-to-be-famous names. Mario Berini, who sang Hoffmann the night I was there, bawled a bit. His alternate, Thomas Hayward, I did not hear.

The cast of *Cosi fan tutte*, as is proper for this work, was equilibrated for volume, beauty of sound, and musicianship, Anne Bollinger, Jane Hobson, and Marilyn Cotlow were the ladies. Joseph Laderoute, Clifford Harvuot, and Lorenzo Alvary were the men. All sang with grace and style, and their concerted numbers were perfection save for being maybe a little louder than that house requires. There were some loud moments in *Hoffmann*, too, but this opera can support an occasional knock-'em-out-of-their-seats effect. Hearing *Cosi* in English, a not at all bad translation by Phyllis and George Mead, gave your prognosticator the idea that a modern-dress production of this lovely and touching work might, if directed with taste, add a certain poignancy to it without the loss of any sparkle. Inconstancy among soldiers' fiancées, after all, is not wholly funny; nor is it, historically speaking, any monopoly of the eighteenth century.

August 1, 1948

Convention in Cleveland

The Music Teachers National Association, meeting in Cleveland during the week of February 24, was the center around which had gathered no less than fifteen other musical organizations. These included the National Association of Schools of Music, the teachers of singing, the choir directors, the string association, the piano teachers, the Matthay Association, the College Music Association, the Accordion Teachers Guild, the Hymn Society of America, the Ohio music teachers, and five musical sororities and fraternities.

The corridors of the Statler Hotel were full of brilliant figures from professional music life—scholars, composers, professors, administrators, executant artists. The publishers were there, too, since these meetings are always accompanied by an exhibit of stocks. No direct sales are made; but musicians constantly pore over the printed music, inspecting, taking notes, listening to everything they would like to use later. There is lots of fraternizing all round; teaching jobs change hands; performances are arranged; contacts, finaglings, and a real exchange of ideas are all part of the intense activity.

Lecture and panel-discussion subjects at these meetings ran from the recondite and technical to such broad but also worrisome matters as how to teach music appreciation in the high schools. All day long in general and in special sessions, theories and experiences were exposed regarding college opera production, ensembles of archaic instruments, the music of ancient Mexico, the psychology of the bow-arm, the performance of Baroque church music, and how many languages should be required of debutant vocalists. A great deal of attention was paid to American composition, to examining the American orchestral, vocal, and pianistic repertory. And numerous short recitals by top American pianists and singers gave evidence of its variety and distinction.

Among the artists performing were Beryl Rubinstein, John Kirkpatrick, Eunice Podis, Denoe Leedy, and the excellent Stanley Quartet. Among the composers played were practically everybody. Particularly impressive to this reporter was a piano recital in which John Kirkpatrick played with love, with poetry, and with a musicianship both impeccable and penetrating American piano works from MacDowell's time to ours. Both pleasing and a shade disappointing was a suave performance of John Verrall's Fourth String Quartet. This work was disappointing for lack of salient profile in the melodic development but infinitely delightful for delicacy of harmonic texture and general workmanship.

Outside the hotel, Cleveland musical establishments offered to the visitors special programs of unusual quality. The Cleveland Orchestra played them a private concert in Severance Hall, including the thirty-year-old *Overture to a Drama* by Arthur Shepherd, still a vigorous and buoyant piece. Edwin Arthur Kraft played them an organ recital at Trinity Episcopal church, where the Kent State University A Cappella Choir also sang contrapuntals from the sixteenth century and modern Russian motets. The music and drama departments of Western Reserve University presented two operas, *Il Maestro di Musica* by Pergolesi and Ralph Vaughan William's *Riders to the Sea*. A concert by the visiting St. Louis Symphony Orchestra added to the general brilliance.

Extra special and quite unique were the preformances of Cleveland's Negro opera company at the Karamu Theater. Established by a settlement house thirty-five years ago, this oldest among America's Negro theaters has recently turned musical. Its director is Benno D. Frank. The repertory, so far, is completely contemporary. Its present program consists of Menotti's *The Medium* and a brand-new German work. The latter is *The Wise Maiden,* a translation of *Die Kluge* by Hans Orff. This work, commented on by your reporter in 1946 from a German radio performance, is one of the most striking examples of the new German declamatory style and of a form which Orff and Boris Blacher have been bringing to perfection in recent years, the radio opera that also makes a theater-piece. The Karamu Theater's performance is the first in this country of any work by Orff.

Hearing everything and seeing everybody at such a gathering of gatherings was not possible to your reviewer. He did not even hear all the music mentioned in this report. But the whole convention, with its fine offerings of music and talk, its assemblage of bright minds, of intellectual, artistic, and administrative personalities, was so rich an experience that he thought it only fair to readers that he should report to them, however summarily, on the high standards of the American musical profession, creative, executant, and pedagogical, as viewed through a cross-section of its leadership.

March 12, 1950

144

Pittsburgh Week End

Finding himself in the city of Pittsburgh, Pennsylvania, last Sunday on other business, your correspondent took a busman's holiday by attending two concerts. He heard the Pittsburgh Symphony Orchestra, conducted by Paul Paray, in the afternoon. And in the evening he went to a concert of the International Society for Contemporary Music, Pittsburgh chapter, at the Carnegie Institute of Technology. The first, a program without any soloist's interference, gave opportunity to hear the distinguished French conductor work in varied styles with an excellent orchestra. The second presented four modern works for violin and piano through the powerful and impeccable hands of Joseph Fuchs and Leo Smit.

The Pittsburgh orchestra has been without a permanent conductor ever since Fritz Reiner left two years ago, but it has not lacked a caretaker. Vladimir Bakaleinikoff, formerly assistant to Mr. Reiner and now listed as Musical Adviser to the orchestra, has gone right on conducting a great many of the concerts. He it is also who makes the necessary replacements every season in personnel, and he it is who keeps the group in training. Guest conductors move in and out, but Mr. Bakaleinikoff goes on. The effectiveness of his regular ministrations is proved but the fact that in spite of having been put through many different kinds of paces for two years by many different star interpreters, the orchestra still plays like an orchestra. It has not fallen, at least not yet, into the splintery string sonorities and faulty general balances that mark the work of habitually guest-conducted groups.

Actually the string body is highly unified in sound and disciplined in technique, the cello and bass sections being particularly notable for power and suavity and the first violins being unusually unanimous of articulation. The woodwinds are excellent, too, and the horns. Trombones and trumpets are a little coarse; the percussion lacks refinement; and I think the brilliant acoustics of the Syria Mosque are not entirely responsible for the stridency of these groups.

But otherwise the orchestra impressed your reviewer as being in good shape, surprisingly good shape.

Paul Paray's program contained, as novelty, Two Dances by Maurice Duruflé, a Parisian organist whose orchestral works, few in number, have not, to my knowledge, been previously played in America. These dances are skillful in harmony, if a shade conservative for France, and ever so charmingly orchestrated. If their expressive content is not strikingly original and their melodic line a bit over-thematic in structure, they are nevertheless Kapellmeistermusik of a delicacy and sophistication that compel the ear.

In Beethoven's *Fidelio* overture Mr. Paray proved once again that the French can play Beethoven without bombast and yet nobly. Similar treatment applied to Brahms has occasionally, as in the readings of this composer by Pierre Monteux, seemed to this reviewer highly valuable as a detergent, or grease remover. Mr. Paray, interpreting Brahms's Third Symphony, gave to its rhythm a lilt and steadiness most advantageous to the architectural line. The expressive line would have been equally enhanced (and was, for the most part) if the conductor had allowed a little more time for those cadences and phrase-endings in which rapidity of harmonic change, or chord-incidence, requires for clarity of hearing a stretching out of the melodic line. Overstretching in such passages has produced the rubbery rhythm and sticky pathos that mar so many contemporary readings of the Brahms symphonies. Mr. Paray's steady progress restores to them serenity and a classic poise; but I do think, now he has got them to moving along again, that a bit more flexibility would give added grace to their lyrical passages. Finesse and delicacy marked his reading of Chabrier's *España*, a work that has regrettably tended to disappear from our programs after long war-horse treatment.

Joseph Fuchs and Leo Smit played that same evening Duos for Violin and Piano by Arthur Berger and Igor Stravinsky and Sonatas for the same combination by Nikolai Lopatnikoff and your reporter. All four works were performed with a technical mastery and a musical authority incomparable. Three of them are relatively familiar and need no comment at this time. The fourth, Lopatnikoff's

Sonata No. 2, was new to your reporter and merits, in his judgment, proclamation. A dissonant neoclassic composition of extended format and high eloquence, it is difficult to play, brilliant, original of sonority, and in every way powerful. What effect it would make when played by artists of lesser skill and understanding I do not know. As played by Mr. Fuchs and Mr. Smit it provoked a favorable audience demonstration rarely accorded to contemporary works. Both the piece and its reception impressed your reviewer as promising a future of some brilliance for this sonata in the repertory of our more courageous recitalists.

It is not hard to understand, mind you. I do not think it would provoke listener resistance unless poorly performed. But virtuosity is of its essence, and any reading of it that was less than perfect technically might fail to communicate its especial delights. On the other hand, a really handsome performance of it gives the double delights of skillful writing and skillful execution. Last Sunday its effect on your reporter was that of a heady mixture. Since the morrow brought no disillusion or bad aftertaste, he would like, if only out of curiosity, to enjoy the experience again, and soon.

April 2, 1950

Modernism in Los Angeles

The Los Angeles region, visited last week end by your correspondent, is an outpost of musical advance on several fronts. Its Philharmonic Orchestra, of which Alfred Wallenstein is conductor, ranked first last season among all the American orchestras in performance of contemporary music. The radio station KFWB has for over a year now offered the local public one of the very few distinguished modern music programs available on the American air. And both the local universities have first-class opera workshops.

Hearing the Los Angeles Philharmonic Orchestra in rehearsal only, since a public concert was not available during his brief stay, your correspondent was particularly impressed by the work of the string section. Woodwinds and brasses, which are likely to be good in all American orchestras, are no less excellent here than elsewhere; but a string section at once so live in sound and so homogeneous in color, so sensitive, so silken, so handsomely drilled and blended for beauty is not to be encountered in more than five or six of our cities. Such a string section, I hardly need add, is where really first-class orchestral work begins.

The radio program mentioned above is called "Music of Today." Its director is Julius Toldi. Its coverage is advanced contemporary composition. It lasts a half hour, beginning at 3 o'clock, Western time, on Sunday afternoons. Its programs consist of all the rarest modern chamber music, and its executions are tops. An interview with the composer of the afternoon is usually offered along with his music, even when this has had to be recorded in some other part of the world and shipped to Los Angeles. I do not know so consistently high-class a program of modern music offered elsewhere on the American air. "Music of Today" is in the class with the Flemish broadcasts of the Belgian National Radio, directed by Paul Collaer, with the B.B.C. Third Program, with the best sent out over the French and Italian national systems.

My attendance at the rehearsal and broadcast of some extremely difficult works of my own, including the ultra-dissonant Sonata da Chiesa, for five disparate instruments, left me gasping with admiration for the executant musicians, for Ingolf Dahl, who conducted, and for, of all people, the Warner Brothers, who own KFWB and who tolerate as a station activity a program of that modernity in presentations of that elegance.

A series of chamber music programs called "Evenings on the Roof," not broadcast, offers at the Wilshire-Ebell Theater conservative modernism and rarish classics in performances of a standard only a shade less high than those of Mr. Toldi's radio program. I heard on one of these one of Reger's sonatas for cello alone and some works of mine, all adequately performed.

148

Both opera workshops were showing that week end. That of U. C. L. A. (the University of California in Los Angeles) had run up as the main number in a concert devoted to my works a scene of some length from *The Mother of Us All*. Presented with piano accompaniment and with only the sketchiest attempt at costuming, it was nevertheless admirably sung and proved again that Jan Popper, the workshop's director, formerly of Stanford University, can make the musical theater communicate under any circumstances.

The University of Southern California happened to be giving a full-dress production of Benjamin Britten's *Albert Herring*. This was professionally led, staged, and framed and would have been acceptable in any professional theater, save for the singing; and even that was merely a little green. The conductor was Wolfgang Martin, formerly of the Metropolitan. The producer and stage director was Carl Ebert, formerly of the Städtische Oper in Berlin and of Glyndebourne. The sets were by Benjamin Grosche. The orchestra was composed of top students and faculty members.

The singers, though not quite ready yet for professional work, were with one exception good singers. Their diction, moreover, their projection of words, a matter of special coaching by William Vennard, was genuinely professional. No Broadway theater offers better; the Metropolitan does not invariably offer as good. If Mr. Martin has not, as a conductor, the infallible dramatic animation of his U. C. L. A. colleague Mr. Popper, he is a thoroughly competent and experienced musical man of the theater. And Carl Ebert is one of the great opera stage directors of all time. With men like this available and with students of good voice as well as good will, both opera workshops in Los Angeles are capable of offering work that is limited in its carrying power only by the essential weaknesses of student singers. A certain rivalry between the two establishments, moreover, seems to help along both. Certainly both are doing distinguished work right now in a field where surely an important part of America's musical future lies. The whole Los Angeles musical scene, I repeat, is full of an awareness of present trends and future opportunities.

Only the film industry lives in and on its own inglorious musical past. That industry, which never has taken a part, any part at all, save perhaps on the trade union front, in either California's or America's intellectual life, has no place in a picture of California's musical life. It has brought musicians to the southern counties, true; but so has the climate. It has given them little work to do worthy of their abilities.

December 18, 1949

Texas's Major Orchestras

The state of Texas, long a center of intercity rivalries, has in recent years added symphonic execution to the fields in which civic emulation is played out before the public. Southern Methodist University, in Dallas, has just staged a music festival, the first in an annual series, between March 15 and 22, in which the Big Three among the Texas symphony orchestras all played for the Dallas public. San Antonio, Houston, and Dallas itself showed off their wares and prowess in Dallas's best auditorium; and critical discussion has been statewide.

There was no jury, no award, no settling of anything. Final opinion seems to have left the orchestras, like the cities themselves, as each unique, each vigorous and full of its own character. It was lately the pleasure of your correspondent to hear all three groups, and not under Dallas conditions but playing in their own ball parks.

The term is not reproachful but almost literally true, since all three orchestras play regularly in convention halls, two of which are commonly used also for sports events. They fill these, too, more often than not. Even without a name soloist for drawing power, any of them is likely to play to an audience of 5,000 or more. Such support is particularly striking in San Antonio, a city of barely 450,000 people, many of whom are Spanish-speaking poor and

150

virtually excluded by this fact from the city's intellectual life. For symphonic attendance, under these conditions, to exceed one per cent of the population is impressive indeed. I do not know the city that can match this devotion to musical art.

To take them in alphabetical order, the Dallas Symphony Orchestra, conducted by Walter Hendl, appeared to this listener as less firmly characterized in its work than the others of the Texas Big Three. This is Mr. Hendl's first year in command of it, and his personnel is not yet firmly set. The group is predominantly first-class; but there are a few spots where changes are indicated and, I believe, planned. The conductor, still in his early thirties, is a musician of unusual preparation, technically and intellectually speaking. He plays the most difficult scores, classic and modern, with clarity and accuracy. He is still learning the repertory, however; and his interpretative powers in the region of the Romantic symphony, which is the center of orchestral repertory, remain a little immature. Also, his ability as a trainer of orchestral musicians has yet to be proved, and probably to be developed, by experience. He makes enlightened programs and plays them cleanly. In modern works he has brilliance and fire. His youth and Americanism endear him to the community. His orchestra, just now, is not quite a homogeneous instrument.

The Houston Symphony Orchestra, conducted by Efrem Kurtz, is a virtuoso group comparable throughout to the northern orchestras. A powerful and solidly blended string body, completed by excellent woodwinds and brasses and topped off by impeccable soloists in all the sections, gives the color range completeness and flexibility. Mr. Kurtz himself, a musician of temperament and culture, is an interpreter, too. His work is brilliant and bright, refined, elegant, and nowhere lacking, either, in that warmth of feeling that gives inner life to classical and Romantic symphonies. His repertory is broad, his style that of a master workman of long experience just now approaching the height of his powers. Having conducted two of his orchestras, in Houston and in Kansas City, this writer can attest to the solidity of their musical training, their discipline, their ability to play anything at any time in any way the conductor sees fit to ask. Houston today is a major orchestra and among the better ones.

The San Antonio Symphony Orchestra is a maverick; there is nothing else quite like it. Founded only ten years ago by Max Reiter, a German-Italian from Trieste, the group has frequently come to national notice through the freshness and distinction of its program policy. What your reporter had not been prepared for is the liveness and loveliness of its playing. The group is young, on the average, and animated by an esprit de corps that reminds one of a football team or a college glee club. It is not a virtuoso orchestra like Houston or Dallas; but it is good throughout, homogeneous, live, lovely and shining. The percussion section is the finest this observer has encountered in any American orchestra. The sound of the whole is silken, suave, translucent. Its recent visit to Dallas produced not only press criticisms and public demonstrations of the highest praise but the honor of an editorial in the Dallas *Morning News.*

All the Texas orchestras play a good deal of American music and encourage Texas composers. San Antonio has also introduced to America a series of postwar works by Richard Strauss, including the *Rosenkavalier* Waltzes and the concert version of *The Legend of Josef,* not yet heard in New York. Next season this composer's last composition, Four Songs for Soprano and Orchestra, will have its American première in San Antonio with Kirsten Flagstad as soloist.

Mr. Reiter and San Antonio have also shown American cities the way to solve their opera problem. An experienced opera conductor both in Germany and in Italy, this director has simply used his own orchestra and an excellent local chorus as the basis of his opera troupe and engaged first-class soloists to complete the cast. He has given operas of Wagner and Strauss not usually possible to regional forces, and he has filled his vast hall at every performance. Two week ends in February constitute at present the season. Four operas, different each year, make up the season's repertory. Air-conditioning of the auditorium will eventually make possible a summer opera season, as well as summer concerts. Skillful financing and the good-will co-operation of trade unions keep deficits down. A similar

152

operation, I am sure, would provide to many another city opera performances of an artistic quality comparable to that now the standard in orchestral concerts. Everybody interested in giving opera to America should take a look at what San Antonio, a South-western city not among our largest or richest, has done.

March 26, 1950

VII. FROM THE U.S.S.R.

Composers in Trouble

The Russians are at it again. First there appears in the left-hand column of *Pravda*'s front page a criticism of the nation's leading composers. They are charged with "formalistic" tendencies, with being influenced by the "decadent" West, with neglect of Russia's "classical" tradition, with failure to maintain the ideals of "socialist realism" and to ennoble as they ought the Russian people. Next the Central Committee of the Communist Party issues a formal denunciation by name and in detail. Next the offending works are removed from the theaters, the symphony concerts, and the radio. Then the composers under attack write open letters to *Pravda* and to the Central Committee thanking them for the spanking, confessing all, and expressing full intention, with the kind advice of the Committee, to reform. After that there is nothing for them to do but "purify" their music, to write new works that will hopefully be in accord with that "new look" that has been the stated ideal of Soviet musicians (and their political leaders) for the last twenty years. Then in a reasonable time they will mostly be back in favor.

For a Soviet composer there is no other solution. Publication and performance being a monopoly of the state, he cannot, nor can any group of composers, operate as a minority appealing to public opinion for justification. Never forget that in Soviet art there is no underground, no unofficial movement, nor, for the present, any possibility of one. This being so, and all observers agree that it is, let us examine, from previous occasions, what is likely to happen to Prokofiev, Shostakovitch, Khachaturian, and company while they remain out of favor.

While Shostakovitch was being disciplined in 1936 and 1937 for the "bourgeois" tendencies that Stalin himself had noticed in *Lady Macbeth of Mzensk*, his works intended for wide consumption were not performed or sold. His chamber music, however, continued to be played and printed; he continued to write it with no alteration of style; and he went on receiving a salary from the Composers' Union. He lived in Moscow, as before, got married, went on working. He was poor and unhappy, drank heavily, we are told by people who visited him; but he was not destitute. He also wrote during this time two symphonies, both of which were rehearsed and performed privately, the last of them only, however, his Fifth, being accepted for public audition. That he had lost no popularity in the meantime was proved by the enormous lines that for three weeks before it was given stood to get seats for the new symphony.

In the case of the literary purge that has been going on since 1936, the majority of those being disciplined have lived in about the same circumstances as Shostakovitch had ten years earlier. Graver cases, however, especially those involving political disaffection or extreme and recalcitrant individualism, have received graver sanctions. Zoschenko, Pasternak, and Akhmatova, for example, were expelled from the Writers' Union. This meant a cutting off of their income and the loss of priority on a Moscow apartment. Until ration cards were abolished it meant also the loss of access to a reasonably nourishing diet. I have not heard of a verified case of a mere writer being sent recently to the Siberian salt mines, as was done with political offenders in the mid-1930's. Expulsion from the Writers' Union (or the Composers' Union) remains, however, a grave form of excommunication, not only for its moral stigma and for the virtual exile from intellectual company but also for the great physical dangers entailed. It has not yet been employed against any of the composers recently denounced.

Whether Shostakovitch and Shebalin, professors at the Moscow Conservatory, will be temporarily retired from their posts I cannot say, though it is rumored that they have already left. Certainly Kharapchenko, the director, has lately been discharged. And it seems likely that Khachaturian, president of the Composers' Union, may find it difficult to remain at that post while under a disciplinary cloud.

What have they done, these composers, to provoke denunciation and disciplinary action? And what moral right has the Central Committee to order their even temporary disgrace? Well, what they have done is to fail, in the judgment of the Party leaders, to conform to the aesthetic of Soviet music in its relation to the whole public, as this was laid down by the musicians themselves back in 1929. That conception is, in our terms, certainly a false one; but it is already an old one, and it is certainly nothing imposed from above. The Russian Association of Proletarian Musicians worked on it for five years before they got it stated the way they wanted it. And though the Association itself was dissolved in 1932, the declaration of 1929 remains to this day the basic aesthetic of Soviet music, of the proper relation of any Soviet composer to decadent "bourgeois" Western culture and to the rising masses of Russia.

In this conception, a composer is an editorial writer. He is supposed to elevate, edify, explain, and instruct. He is to speak a language both comprehensible to all and worthy by its dignity of a nation-wide public. He is to avoid in technique the overcontra-

156

puntal and the overharmonic, in expression the abstract, the tricky, the mystical, the mechanical, the erotic. He is to turn his back on the West and make Russian music for Russia, for all of Russia, and for nothing beyond. His consecration to this aim is to be aided and reinforced by public criticism, as well as by the private counsels of his colleagues. Judgment as to the accomplishment of the aim is not, however, his privilege nor that of his critics. That belongs to the Communist Party, which has the responsibility for leadership and guidance in artistic as in all other matters. The composers, in other words, have determined their own ideal and accepted, along with the ideals and forms of the society in which they live and work and which they have helped toward the achievement of its present internal solidity, the principle that the professional body alone, and still less the listening public, is not the final judge of music's right to survive.

This idea is not in accord with our Western concept of the integrity of the professions. Nevertheless, it is that of the Soviet government and of all, so far as we know, Soviet musicians. The hasty *mea culpa* of the Soviet artist in trouble with the Central Committee shocks the Western mind, but I see no reason to doubt its sincerity. Seven of the boys are in a jamb right now, and I suspect most of them will get out of it. I sincerely hope they will, because they are good composers and because I like to see good composers writing and getting played and published. Myself I have never taken much stock in Soviet music. I am too individualistic to like the idea of an artist's being always a servant of the same set-up, even of so grand a one as a great people organized into a monolithic state. I don't like monolithic states anyway; they remind me of the great slave-owning empires of antiquity.

But my tastes are not involved in the matter. Soviet music is the kind of music that it is because the Soviet composers have formally and long ago decided to write it that way, because the Communist party accepts it that way, and because the people apparently take it. When the Party clamps down on it for "deviation," who am I to complain if the composers of it themselves don't? Whether they could do so with any hope of success, of course, is doubtful. All we know from previous occasions is that he who confesses and reforms quickest gets off the lightest. I do not find, given the whole of Russian political and aesthetic theory, that the procedure is undignified; and apparently the composers do not find it so, however much they may regret having to submit to the sanctions. It seems likely that they would feel far worse, even if they could survive, excommunicated from the intellectual life and deprived of their forum.

Russians mostly, I imagine, believe in their government and country. Certainly these great, official public figures do. They could not, in so severe and censored a period, have become national composers by mere chicanery. That is not what bothers me about them. Nor yet that they are always getting into trouble from excess of musical fancy. What worries me, and has for twenty years, is that, for all their devotion, noble precepts, faith in their fatherland, and extraordinary privileges, their music, judged by any standard, is no better than it is. I only hope, against all reason and probability, that a similar preoccupation on the part of the Central Committee is at least a little bit responsible for the present disciplinary action. Russian music may or may not need ideological "purification." But it certainly needs improvement.

February 22, 1948

Soviet Aesthetics

The formal censuring of Russia's eight top composers by the Central Committee of the Communist Party, an action that seems to have caused no less excitement in the Soviet Union than in the West, continues to be explained, defended, and insisted upon by dignitaries of Soviet musical life. At the recently held Congress of Soviet

Composers there were innumerable speeches of apology and exhortation, confessions of backsliding, further denunciations, preachments, protests, and ukases from on high. The whole effect, to an outsider at some distance, is reminiscent at once of those interminable conversations about the state of somebody's soul that abound in Dostoevsky and of a revivalist camp meeting. Certainly the boys are worried about themselves and about one another.

The present outsider is under no illusion that aesthetic matters would be handled any more convincingly in his own country by a committee made up of either Democratic or Republican party chiefs or by a consortium of concert managers and publicity agents or by any other group among us that might be animated by an itch to use music and the public's enjoyment of it for its own purposes. It is probable, even, that a congress of American composers, held under a similar emergency, would show a not inconsiderable amount of conformist sentiment and also that some of the resistant spirits would remain shamefully (if sagaciously) silent. All the same, the Russian spectacle is entertaining, more so, indeed, to this observer than a great deal of the music that it is all about. And little by little one gets an inkling of what it is the Party in Russia has on its mind, musically speaking.

The magazine *Sovietskoye Iskusstvo* (*Soviet Art*) published on February 28 of this year articles by Tikhon Khrennikov and Marion Koval that, for all the carefully routined phrasing of their indignation, here and there let the cat out of the bag. The former, moderately well known here as a symphonist, has lately replaced Aram Khachaturian as president of the Society of Soviet Composers. The latter is music editor of *Soviet Art* and president of the State Music Publishing Committee for the selection of works to be printed. Both use the word *formalist* (or, rather, its Russian equivalent) as a term of intense reproach and join it regularly for emphasis with the adjectives *Western* and *decadent*. Both have some difficulty defining formalist tendencies, but both insist that when a work's subject matter is not clear to all formalism is present. Wherever the subject matter is frivolous, pessimistic, or "unhealthy" it is also assumed to exist, though its running mate, the word *decadence*, is more easily comprehensible to us in that connection.*

In Soviet aesthetics, however, undesirable subjects and sentiments are assumed to be inseparable from "formalistic" expression. And "formalistic" expression (also equatable with "individualistic") is recognizable in music by excessive dissonance, harsh instrumentation, unusual instrumentations (of a kind not available in provincial orchestras), percussive instrumentation, too much counterpoint, "linearity" in general, slow tempos, failure to employ folklore themes, the distortion of folklore themes, failure to follow "classic" models, distortion of classic models, and the use of any device or texture for its intrinsic interest rather than for directly expressive purposes. For critics unskilled in musical analysis, subject matter, where clear, is apparently sufficient basis for judgment, since sound subjects are assumed to make for sound musical expression, just as "decadent" subjects make for "decadent-formalistic" (add "Western" and "bourgeois") expression. The work which set off the recent troubles, however—Muradeli's opera *The Great Friendship*—is one in which the subject, Stalin's years with Lenin, is obviously both a noble one, in Russia, and one extremely touchy to handle. Composing it, or even reviewing it, is a major hazard.

Miss Koval attacks the music critics for not having, since 1936, kept Shostakovitch in line and utters a clarion call for the reorganization of musical science, musicology, and music criticism, that these may all be turned "without losing a single day" "to the fulfillment of tasks laid down by the historical decision of the Party." All this is plain enough as an order, though the constant testing of music for "formalist-decadent" tendencies seems a delicate operation and one for which the intellectual instruments available are far from exact. Perhaps musical science, musicology, and criticism are supposed to set about perfecting these. In any case, Miss Koval warns the critics who used to admire Shostakovitch, but recently haven't dared, that they have done a U-turn once too often. They should

* The Russian word translated as "formalism" seems to mean something like "form*u*lism," that is to say, composition by means of stock formulas, technical or expressive.

160

have anticipated the Party's decision instead of being caught by it riding on a wrong bandwagon. The critic is thus conceived not as a reporter but as a mentor "expressing the opinion of the Soviet public," an instrument of the Party actually, a beacon light and a fog horn, warning everybody constantly against writing for the intellectual group. Beauty without distinction, a nonsensical concept to the Western mind, is apparently the present ideal in Russia.

Mr. Khrennikov purports to give, in his article on *Formalism and Its Roots*, the story of how modern music went wrong. This he traces, in Russia, back to the period of political reaction that followed the unsuccessful revolutionary uprisings of 1905. Serge de Diaghilev is an agent of evil in this picture, Stravinsky and Prokofiev being his tools. But perhaps I had better quote the composer's own words (in a translation which I owe to the courtesy of our State Department).

"Diaghilev openly called on Russian artists to serve an apprenticeship with the modern West. The modernist movement in Russian music is thus closely linked with frank servility before the Western musical market."

"The basic aim pursued by the authors of these works [Stravinsky's *Petrouchka*, *Rite of Spring*, and *Les Noces*, Prokofiev's *Scythian Suite* and *Chout*] is to withdraw from the contemporary human world into the world of abstraction."

"In *Petrouchka* and *Les Noces* Stravinsky, with Diaghilev's blessing, uses Russian folk customs in order to mock at them in the interest of European audiences, which he does by emphasizing Asiatic primitivism, coarseness, and animal instincts and by deliberately introducing sexual motives."

"In Hindemith's *Saint Susan* religious eroticism is shown in revoltingly naturalistic detail. Similarly pathological are the neuropathic operas of Alban Berg and, in recent times, especially *The Medium* by Gian-Carlo Menotti, which has scored a great success with the bourgeois public of America. The central character of this opera is a woman who is a professional spiritist and faker, a dipsomaniac, and a murderer to boot."

"The operas of . . . Hindemith, Krenek, Alban Berg . . . Britten

. . . and Menotti are mere concatenations of hideous sounds marked by complete disregard of natural human singing. This music openly harks back to the primitive barbaric cultures of prehistoric society and extols the eroticism, psychopathic mentality, sexual perversion, amorality, and shamelessness of the twentieth-century bourgeois hero."

"Olivier Messiaen, according to his own statement, draws his creative inspiration from ecclesiastical books and from the works of medieval Catholic scholastics such as Thomas Aquinas."

"Igor Stravinsky, apostle of the reactionary forces in bourgeois music, creates a Catholic Mass in conventional-decadent style [a work Mr. Khrennikov cannot have heard, since it is still unpublished and unperformed] or circus jazz pieces, with equal indifference."

"Among the works of Soviet composers of the twenties and thirties that offer numerous instances of formalistic tendencies are: Shostakovitch's opera *The Nose,* his 2d and 3d Symphonies; Prokofiev's ballets *The Prodigal Son, On the Dnieper, Steel Leap,* his opera *Fiery Angel,* 3d and 4th Symphonies, 5th Piano Concerto, and 5th Sonata for Piano; Mossolov's *Iron Foundry* and *Newspaper Advertisements;* Knipper's operas *North Wind* and *Tales of a Plaster Buddha;* Deshevov's opera *Ice and Steel;* Miaskovsky's 10th and 13th Symphonies, 3d and 4th Piano Sonatas; S. Feinberg's piano sonatas and 1st Piano Concerto; Shebalin's *Lenin* Symphony and 2d Symphony; G. Popov's 1st Symphony; B. Lyatoshinsky's 2d Symphony and songs; I. Belza's 1st and 2d Symphonies, also his songs; L. Polovinkin's *Telescope* for orchestra and *Incidents* for piano; G. Litinsky's quartets and sonatas; V. Shcherbachov's 3d Symphony; and so forth."

"Formalist tendencies received their most striking expression in the opera *Lady Macbeth of Mzensk,* by Shostakovitch, and in his ballet *The Luminous Brook,* both of which were flatly condemned in the articles of *Pravda,* published in 1936, when *Pravda* acting on instructions of the Central Committee of the Communist Party, exposed the harm and danger of the formalist school for the future of Soviet music."

As I said before, the maneuvers are not wholly clear, but it would seem that the Russians are trying to do two things. One is to limit music to its possible uses as an arm of the state's social policy. Many governments have tried this at one time or another. The idea is not a new one, but the history of its success is meager. The other effort is to create a nonexplosive, a foolproof kind of art, a beauty with no "strangeness in the proportion." This is not a new idea either, although precedent for its success is, to my knowledge, nonexistent. On both counts the talented boys have reason to be worried.

May 2, 1948

Russians Recover

Dmitri Shostakovitch, the most popular of living Russian composers, inside the Soviet Union or out, has apparently been reinstated in the favor of the Politburo. A year ago he had been removed from that favor, along with five other well known composers—Prokofiev, Khachaturian, Miaskovsky, Shebalin, and Popov. He had also been removed, along with some of these others, from public office. Shostakovitch and Miaskovsky ceased to teach composition at the Moscow Conservatory. Shebalin was replaced as head of that institution by A. Sveshnikov, a choral conductor. Khachaturian lost to Tikhon Khrennikov the position of Secretary General of the Union of Soviet Composers. He also ceased to be head of its Orgkomitet, or organizing committee. This group, working in close collaboration with the Committee on Arts of the Ministry of Education, has huge power, since it decides what works will be printed and recommends works for performance to opera houses, symphony orchestras, and touring virtuosos.

Prokofiev, who did not teach or hold any official post, was ostracized by the simple means of removing nearly all his works from the opera and concert repertories. The same measure was applied, of course, to the other purged composers, but less drastically. Shostakovitch's First and Fifth symphonies, Miaskovsky's Symphony on White-Russian Themes, Khachaturian's Cello Concerto, and divers other pieces by the denounced "formalists" have gone right on being played, at least occasionally, since the purge.

Last year's offense, let us recall, was not the first for Shostakovitch. Back in 1936 he had been subjected to disciplinary measures of a similar nature lasting a year and a half. His chief offense had been the opera *Lady Macbeth of Mzensk* and his work of restitution the Fifth Symphony. This time the troublesome piece was his Ninth Symphony; and his comeback has been accomplished through two film scores, *The Young Guard* and *Michurin*. The first of these is a heroic and optimistic melodrama about the exploits of the Komsomol during the defense of the Don Basin. The other is a biography in color of a Soviet hero, I. V. Michurin, founder of Soviet anti-Mendelian biology. Though neither film has yet reached the Stanky Theater, they have passed the musical judges; and two musical excerpts from *The Young Guard* have been printed in *Sovietskaya Muzyka* of October, 1948.

The cases of Khachaturian and Shostakovitch are simpler than that of Prokofiev. The former's "illness," as the Russians like to refer to any artistic deviation, is only recently contracted and is 50 per cent non-musical, anyway. This half is a result of his political position. As a Party member, president of the Orgkomitet, and Secretary General of the Composers' Union, he was naturally held responsible for whatever protection the "formalists" had enjoyed prior to their denunciation. A first offender, a man of charming personality, and a convinced Bolshevik from the periphery of the Union (Armenia), he represents to the Politburo the achievements of a national-culture policy dear to its initiator Stalin. Of all the purged six, he has been the most played since his purge. As a Party member, he has continued, moreover, to serve on Union subcommittees. Professor T. Livanova (sole woman member of the Presidium of the Composers' Union) dealt with him indulgently in the July, 1948, number of *Sovietskaya Muzyka*. His successor as Secretary General of the Composers' Union, T. Khrennikov, also patted him on the back (for effort) in his "state of the Union" message of January 1, 1949.

If Khachaturian appears now as on his way out of trouble, Prokofiev seems to be in no such position. Not a product of Soviet culture but of the pre-revolutionary Czarist regime, a traveled man long resident in such centers of "bourgeois corruption" as Paris and the U.S.A., an associate of the Russian émigré enterprise, Serge de Diaghilev's Ballet Russe, and a resident of the Soviet Union only since 1933, this composer is being referred to more and more in the Soviet press as an incorrigible case. The recently deceased Boris Asafiev, Acting President of the Composers' Union (Stalin being Honorary President), also Khrennikov and Marion Koval, editor of *Sovietskaya Muzyka* and a party-line whip, have all denounced him. Consistently and, one surmises, deliberately nowadays, his name is linked with such "servile and corrupt musical businessmen" as Stravinsky, such "degenerate, blackguard, anti-Russian lackeys of the Western bourgeoisie" as Diaghilev. His latest opera, moreover, composed under the purge, has been found unacceptable.

The latter, based on a story by Boris Polyevoi and entitled *The Life of a Real Person* (libretto by the composer's second wife, Mira Mendelssohn), deals with a Soviet flier and hero who lost both legs in the war. In December of last year the conductor Khaikin, who seems to admire Prokofiev deeply, organized in Leningrad a public reading of the opera. He apparently overstepped in this case his prerogatives, for the Leningrad papers scolded him severely; and Khrennikov called the incident "a fatal one for Prokofiev." Khrennikov specified further that "this opera shows that the traditions of Western modernism have captivated his consciousness." Moreover, "To him an acute dramatic situation is an end in itself; and the overplay of naturalistic details seems more important than the creation of musically truthful and convincing images of a Soviet hero with his life-asserting, ebullient will and his bold outlook into the future." Khrennikov also regrets that Prokofiev did not submit the work to his comrade-composers for criticism before its unfortunate concert hearing. The critic of *Izvestya*, Mr. Kukharski, dismisses the piece as "impractical, ivory-tower workmanship" and the composer

as "an artist who has severed all connections with real Soviet life."
Pravda thinks it "doubtful" whether one "can expect anything to
satisfy the needs of the great Soviet people" from a "composer whose
work is penetrated to the core" by "Western formalist decay."

In contrast to the apparently incurable maladjustments of Prokofiev (who is physically ill, as well, for he seems to have had last
spring another stroke like the one he suffered in 1946), Shostakovitch
is clearly on the road to recovery. Not only is he being sent to us
on a mission; he has also been praised by the head of his union for
his "successful" film music. His position last year was grave. As a
second offender he might easily have lost his apartment. Koval
actually suggested at a Composers' Union meeting as late as last
October that those afflicted with "decadent, bourgeois tendencies . . .
could very profitably move out of Moscow to the periphery of the
vast Soviet land and get their inspiration from a close contact with
the life of the people in the provinces, in collective farms and fac-
tories." Happily, however, Mr. Shostakovitch encountered nothing
so drastic as forced residence on the "periphery" of the Soviet
Union.* His case was argued in the magazines; his confession was
accepted at face value; his penitential work has been judged good.
And so (the United States willing) he is going to be sent to visit us.

Koval has analyzed his chronic "illness" as follows. Shostakovitch's
great natural gift has been perverted by:

1. Discordant German counterpoint (presumably the Hindemith
style).

2. Introducing into the "sacred soil of the pure classic Russian
tradition jazz neurosis and Stravinskyan rhythmical paroxysms."

3. Inability to write "singable" melodic lines.

4. Naturalistic approach to subject matter. (The love scene in
Lady Macbeth shocked some here, too.)

5. "Limitless adulation of a chorus of sycophants" (in other
words, success).

He can, however, be cured by the following regimen:

1. Avoiding "dissonance."

* By "periphery of the Soviet Union" many Russians understand Siberia.

2. Avoiding any harmonic syntax more advanced than that of the late Sergei Rachmaninov.

3. Learning to write "easy" tunes.

4. Avoiding dependence on "abstract" instrumental and symphonic forms.

5. Writing more songs.

6. Strictly abstaining from jazz rhythms, paroxystic syncopation, "fake" (meaning dissonant) polyphony, and atonality.

7. Writing operas about Soviet life.

8. Turning his attention in general to the song of the great Soviet people and forgetting about the West.

Whether sending him to visit the West is the best way to make him forget about it is not for a mere Westerner to judge. Certainly his Western admirers will give him an unforgettable welcome. But before we submit him to the temptations of a bourgeois publicity-apotheosis, let us remember him as last described from home sources, piously glorifying Soviet science. In *Pravda*'s art magazine of January 1, 1949, he is mentioned as having written successful music for a charming episode in the film *Michurin*. The biologist is therein described as "standing high above a blooming apple tree and in total self-oblivion conducting a rapturous, wordless chorus of the Voices of Nature." "These Voices," it is added, "have been clearly heard and well expressed by the composer." Hollywood itself could not, I am sure, provide a musician with a more glorious opportunity than the scene here described; nor could any composer wish for a more auspicious way to salute the U.S., hereditary home of "formalistic decadence," than by indulgence in such unashamed hamming.

The above, or, rather, the information contained in it, is derived from a report of some length on the Russian musical press, furnished me, with translations, by the composer Nicholas Nabokov. I regret that space restrictions forbid more extensive quotations from this entertaining material, but I think I have incorporated faithfully the gist of it.

February 27, 1949

VIII. REFLECTIONS

The Intellectual Audience (I)

Anyone who attends musical and other artistic events eclectically must notice that certain of these bring out an audience thickly sprinkled with what are called "intellectuals" and that others do not. It is managements and box offices that call these people intellectuals; persons belonging to that group rarely use the term. They are a numerous body in New York, however, and can be counted on to patronize certain entertainments. Their word-of-mouth communication has an influence, moreover, on public opinion. Their favor does not necessarily provoke mass patronage, but it does bring to the box office a considerable number of their own kind, and it does give to any show or artist receiving it some free advertising. The intellectual audience in any large city is fairly numerous, well organized, and vocal.

This group, that grants or withholds its favor without respect to paid advertising and that launches its ukases with no apparent motivation, consists of people from many social conditions. Its binding force is the book. It is a reading audience. Its members may have a musical ear or an eye for visual art, and they may have neither. What they all have is some acquaintance with ideas. The intellectual world does not judge a work of art from the talent and skill embodied in it; only professionals judge that way. It seeks in art a clear connection with contemporary aesthetic and philosophic trends, as these are known through books and magazines. The intellectual audience is not a professional body; it is not a professors' conspiracy, either, nor a publishers' conspiracy. Neither is it quite a readers' anarchy. Though it has no visible organization, it forms its own opinions and awards its own prizes in the form of free advertising. It is a very difficult group to maneuver or to push around.

In New York it is a white-collar audience containing stenographers, saleswomen, union employees of all kinds, many persons from the comfortable city middle-aged middle class, and others from the suburban young parents. There are snappy dressers, too, men and women of thirty who follow the mode, and artists' wives from downtown who wear peasant blouses and do their own hair. Some are lawyers, doctors, novelists, painters, musicians, professors. Even the carriage trade is represented, and all the age levels above twenty-five. A great variety of costume is always present, of faces and figures with character in them. Many persons of known professional distinction give it seasoning and tone.

The presence of such an audience at a musical event is no result of paid advertising or of standard publicity. Its representation is small at the Metropolitan Opera, the Philharmonic, and the concerts of the N.B.C. Symphony Orchestra, though it will go to all these places for special works. Dimitri Mitropoulos, for example, drew a brilliant audience for his recent performance at the Philharmonic of Strauss's *Elektra*. The smaller symphonic ensembles, the City

Center opera, the New Friends of Music, and the League of Composers bring out lots of intellectuals. So do certain ballet performances and the spectacles of Martha Graham, though not, on the whole, for musical reasons. The International Society for Contemporary Music, the Composers' Forum, concerts and opera productions at the Juilliard School and at Columbia University, and certain recitalists are definitely favored. Wanda Landowska, harpsichord players in general, Jennie Tourel, Maggie Teyte, Martial Singher, Gold and Fizdale, sometimes Josef Szigeti are all notable for the interest they offer to persons of high mental attainments.

The conductors chiefly favored by this group are Reiner, Monteux, and Ansermet. The intellectuals often come in a body to hear them. They come individually from time to time to hear Toscanini, Koussevitzky, Bernstein. They have shown no consistent interest in Rodzinski, Mitropoulos, Munch, Ormandy, or in recent years Stokowski. Beecham's audience appeal, for all his high cultural equipment, remains strictly musical, though his recordings are collected by many persons from other professions.

Flagstad, too, is a purely musical phenomenon; and so is Horowitz. The latter, indeed, no longer pleases wholly even the musical world, if I read his public right. One sees fewer and fewer known musicians at his recitals, more and more a public clearly not familiar with standard piano repertory. The music world attends en masse Landowska, Schnabel, and Curzon. The last two, however, have never made full contact with the world called intellectual, the world of verbalized ideas and general aesthetic awareness.

Management's aim is to mobilize the ticket-buying and propaganda power of this world without alienating the mass public. The latter is respectful of intellectual opinion, which it learns about through the magazines of women's wear, but resistant to the physical presence of the intellectual audience. The varieties of fancy dress and interesting faces, the pride of opinion expressed in overheard conversations, the clannish behavior of these strange and often monstrous personalities are profoundly shocking to simpler people. Their behavior expresses both a freedom of thought and a degree of ostentation that are not available to the standardized consumer. Much as he would like to enjoy everything that is of good report, he is really most comfortable among his own kind listening to Marian Anderson. This is why the Philharmonic and the Metropolitan managements make little or no play for the intellectual trade and discourage efforts in that direction from the musical wing. They have a mass public of sorts already, do not need intellectual promotion. They seem to fear, moreover, that intellectual influence, bearing always toward the left in program-making, may keep away more paying customers than it brings in.

Beneath all of management's dealings with the intellectual group lie two assumptions. One is that intellectuals like novelty and modernity. The other is that the mass public dislikes both. I think the first is true. I doubt the second. I am more inclined to believe, from long acquaintance with all sorts of musical publics, that it is management which dislikes novelty and everything else that inter- feres with standardization. I suspect that management's design is toward conditioning the mass public to believe that it dislikes novelty. Some success has already been achieved in this direction. If intellectual opinion has any carrying power beyond the centers of its origin, there is a job to be done, a war to be fought across the nation. The intellectuals' own survival, even, may depend on winning it. For unless these bright ones carry some weight in the forming of everybody's opinions and tastes, they are a useless body and can be by-passed by any power-group that wants to use art for its own ends.

January 15, 1950

The Intellectual Audience (II)

Musical programs of a standard character, no matter how polished their execution, appeal chiefly to an audience of musicians and music lovers, in other words, of persons capable of emotional satisfaction through the ear. Musical programs of an unusual character often bring into the concert hall another public. This public, liberally salted, as I mentioned last Sunday, with persons distinguished in other arts and professions, is commonly referred to as the intellectual audience. The term is accurate, because intellectual curiosity rather than an appetite for auditory experience is the reason for its being there. This audience is the element that gives to New York, Paris, Vienna, and London their power as centers of musical influence. There is nothing provincial, musically speaking, about any city where the intellectual audience is large.

Many artists and most managements, certainly those whose aim is the standardization of repertory and execution, would like to dispense with this audience, to trade entirely in musical skill and prestige. It is not possible to do so, because the musical press, which no artist or institution can do without, speaks at least half the time from an intellectual, an aesthetic, a trends-and-general-ideas point of view. Individuals can avoid contact with this kind of criticism, or at least minimize the injurious effects of it on their careers, only by keeping away from the musical centers. Nelson Eddy, Jeanette MacDonald, and formerly Oscar Levant have long followed a provincial career. Others have risked occasional criticism from the New York press for the sake of acquiring institutional prestige, since for radio appearances and some of the touring trade, singing occasionally at the Metropolitan Opera in leading roles provides a substitute for intellectual prestige. Risë Stevens, Gladys Swarthout, Lily Pons, Robert Merrill, and James Melton have followed this line, appearing occasionally in opera here but avoiding as frequently as possible the risks of the midtown solo recital.

Institutions cannot so easily by-pass the press and its power of dispensing intellectual prestige. The nonprofit-making ones need such prestige to raise money. The others—the radio, television, and gramophone companies—need it for public good will, for silencing criticism of their business operations. They all need it for advertising, because the musical press of New York is one of the chief channels of communication between the intellectual world of music,

172

which forms opinion, and the mass public, which buys tickets. This does not mean that all the New York critics are spokesmen for the intellectual world. Some are and some are not. Only that part of the press which defends intellectual opinion against management's conservatism and the inertia of mass receptivity is an intellectual press. The rest is either a low-brow press or an agent of the music business. There is no such thing as a purely musical press, one which reviews only from an auditory point of view, because it is not possible to write about music without thinking about it, or to think about it without taking some position with regard to contemporary aesthetics.

The professional music world itself has little interest in intellectual criticism. It makes up its mind on technical grounds, is suspicious of aesthetics, of all talk about trends and general ideas. Political and religious agencies that patronize music are interested only in trends and general ideas. That is why patronage from these sources always involves either institutional propaganda or something clearly denominable as education. All criticism in such cases, unless favorable, is definitely unwelcome. The intellectual world, on the other hand, the free association of all those who read books, loves to read criticism. It finds the critical columns a battle ground of ideas, a track meet of polemical skills, a festival of intellectual exercise in every way stimulating. Indeed, it follows music far more consistently through reading music reviews than through attendance at musical events.

The intellectual audience wants culture with its music, wants information, historical perspectives, enlarged horizons. It demands of program makers constant experiment and a huge variety. It is far more interested in repertory, as a matter of fact, than in execution. It tends to envisage the whole of music as a vast library in which everything is available, or should be. The strictly musical audience and the mass public are more easily satisfied. They think of the concert life as a sort of boarding house where you take what is offered and don't reach. Their good nature is easily abused by managements and other organizing agencies. The intellectuals are more demanding and refuse to be spoon fed. That is why, as a musician, I value the intellectual element in audiences.

The intellectual world needs us musicians, of course, too. Without some acquaintance of the allied arts, the book-reading public is just a part of the book trade, as the music world, by itself, is only a branch of the entertainment industry. Or worse, a herd of sheep being fattened on propaganda. Propaganda is all right if it is your own. Otherwise it has no place in culture, any more than industrialized entertainment has. There will always be plenty of those around, anyway. What the world needs most just now, beyond food and clothing, is art in the classical sense of the term. In that meaning it is neither propaganda nor entertainment, though it can use both for its own purpose, which is the representation of an inner or outer reality.

I think we need not fear communicating realities to the mass public. I also believe that musicians have reason to welcome, in the process of perfecting for this purpose their communicative powers, not only the criticism of other musicians and music lovers but also the more intellectual response of all those who, without being specifically music-minded, are in their own practice occupied with reality and find pleasure in the constant search for convincing transcripts of it.

January 22, 1950

The Problem of Sincerity

If art is a form of communication, and music the form of art best suited to the communication of sentiments, feelings, emotions, it does seem strange that the clear communication of these should be beset with so many difficulties. Perfection of the technical amenities, or at least an approach to it, is more commonly to be met with in

174

the concert hall than is a convincing interpretation of anything. They play and sing so prettily, these recitalists, work so hard and so loyally to get the notes of the music right that it is a matter of constant astonishment to me how few of them can make it speak.

Composers, too, have trouble communicating, especially American composers. They make you great, big, beautiful, shapely structures; but it is not always clear what purpose, with regard to living, these are intended to fulfill. One has a strange feeling sometimes, right in the middle of a concert season, that the music world, both the composers and their executants, are just a swarm of busy ants, accomplishing nothing to human eyes but carrying grains of sand back and forth. How much useful work anybody is doing, of course, is hard to know. But seldom, O, so seldom, does a musical action of any kind speak clearly, simply, without detours.

Part of this inefficiency comes, I am sure, from the prestige of Romantic attitudes in a nonromantic age. From the violinist in a Russian restaurant who hopes to be tipped for pushing his violin into your shashlik to the concert pianist who moons over the keys or slaps at them in a seeming fury, all are faking. They are counterfeiting transports that they do not have and that in nine cases out of ten are not even the subject of the music. For music of passionate and personal expressivity is a small part indeed of standard repertory. There is a little of it, though very little, in Mozart, a bit more in Beethoven, some in Mendelssohn, a great deal in Schumann and Chopin, less in Brahms, and then practically no more at all till you get to Bartók. Its presence in Bruckner and Mahler, though certain, is obscured by monumental preoccupations. Berlioz, Liszt and Wagner, Strauss and Schönberg, even Debussy and the modernists operate mostly on a level of complexity that prevents an efficient interpreter from going too wild and the meaning from getting too private. It is not that technical difficulties prevent introversion. But the simple fact that the subject of most music is evocation obliges both composer and executant to objective procedures.

Music of personal lyricism, Schumann, for instance, can be played or sung without antics and often is. But it cannot be rendered convincingly without personal involvement. This poses the problem of sincerity. You can write or execute music of the most striking evocative power by objective methods, provided you have an active imagination. You can represent other people's emotions, as in the theater, by the same means, plus decorum. But you cannot project a personal sentiment that you do not have. If you fake it knowingly, you are dramatizing that which should be transmitted directly; and if you fake it unknowingly, you are merely, by deceiving yourself, attempting to deceive your audience.

Sincerity is not a requisite for theatrical work, for evocative work, for any music that is, however poetic, objective in character. Taste, intelligence, and temperament are the only requirements. These will enable you to get into any role and out of it again, to perform it perfectly, to communicate through it. They are not sufficient for a proper rendering of Schumann's songs or of the Bartók quartets. These you must feel. What gives to lieder recitals and string quartet concerts their funereal quality, when they don't come off, and their miraculous excitement, when they do, is the absence or presence of authentic feeling in the interpretation.

Any sincerely felt reading must be a personal one. Objective music has, more often than not, traditional readings that are correct. All traditional readings of the music of personalized sentiment are, by definition, incorrect. Because sentiments, feelings, private patterns of anxiety and relief are not subject to standardization. They must be spontaneous to have any existence at all, spontaneous and unique. Naturally, experienced persons can teach the young many things about the personalized repertory. But there is no set way it must be rendered, and any attempt to impose one on it takes the life out of it. The exactly opposite condition obtains regarding objective music. This benefits enormously from exact procedures and standardized renderings, from every thoughtful observance and precision. Personal involvement with it, the injection of sentiment, is a great foolishness.

The whole question of sincerity hangs on a difference between those feelings with which one can become temporarily identified by imagination and those which are one's own and relatively permanent. The former, which make for drama, constitute nine-tenths of the whole musical repertory and nine-tenths of any mature composer's available subject matter. Mixing the two kinds gets nobody anywhere. Treating personal music objectively gives a pedantic effect. Treating objective music personally gives a futile effect. Nevertheless, on account of the prestige that historical Romanticism enjoys, the latter procedure dominates our concert halls. All over America artists are endeavoring to treat the repertory, the vast body of which is objective music, and composers are treating the monumental forms, too, as if their personal fantasies about these were a form of communication. On the other hand, more often than not they treat personal music to a routined and traditional streamlining that prevents it altogether from speaking that language of the heart that is speech at all only when it comes from the heart. They should leave the stuff alone unless they are capable of spontaneity. Once rid of their romantic pretenses, too, they would certainly do better with the rest of the repertory. For composers the urgency is even greater. Let them do theater and evocations to their hearts' content. But in the domain of private feelings, fooling around with those one does not have is suicidal.

February 8, 1948

Tradition Today

An ideal orchestral conductor, in the last century, was one who pleased first the musical public and second those persons in the audience whose musical attainments were of a modest character. In those days the aim was public instruction. Hence it was of prime importance that the music be played right. If in addition it could be made attractive, that was luck. Nowadays, with philanthropic subsidies diminished and management, for box-office reasons, firmly in the saddle, the aim of our orchestras is first to please a large ticket-buying public and only second to preserve the traditions of interpretation as these have been handed down and to renew them in full knowledge of their existing state.

We have, as a result, two kinds of conductors, the traditionals and the independents, the former representing a knowledgeable approach, the latter a highly personalized ability to hold attention. The former group is dominated in the United States by Fritz Reiner and Pierre Monteux. The leaders of the other tendency are Leopold Stokowski and Serge Koussevitzky. The enormous prestige of Toscanini is due, I think, not to any gift for combining the personal with the impersonal but to the mercurial speed with which, from work to work and even from phrase to phrase, he can oscillate between them. His application of a theaterlike objectivity to the concert stage is in no sense a preservation of tradition. He has, in fact, blithely broken with as many sound survivals as he has of outworn usages. His concert readings are neither strictly personal nor strictly impersonal, though they are aimed, I think, at impersonality. In the theater, however, he is impersonal and at all times aware of tradition, its nature and necessary reinvigoration.

Managements often refer to tradition-minded conductors as "technicians" and to the independents as "interpreters." As a matter of fact, the Stokowskis and Koussevitzkys of this world are no less skillful at attaining their musical ends than are the others. They are first-class disciplinarians and justly renowned as trainers of the young. Technicians they certainly are. Interpretation, indeed, is their weaker side. What they rarely do, in any clear meaning of the term, is to interpret, or translate, the known sense of a piece. They improvise it, rather. Their appeal, for musicians and for nonmusicians, is one of sheer technique, of pure beauty in sound. They give offense, when they do, only on grounds of taste. They do not always know, or greatly care, about the exact character, so far as this is known to musicians, of a given work in repertory. The traditionalists do know this, are aware, at least, that the interpretation of music is not entirely a matter of personal fancy and of skill in manipulating crowd psychology.

This is not to say that tempos, accents, and rhythmic inflections are easily ascertainable. If they were, any musician could be a great interpreter. They demand both thought and study. They demand above all, if they are to be convincing to other people who have put thought and study on matters musical, to be arrived at in full knowledge of what these have been in the memory of living lovers of music. One does not expect, moreover, that executants should follow a model precisely. One expects them to preserve tradition by violating it, to clarify it by weeding out the merely habitual, to correct it, to add to it their own enlightenment. Copying one's predecessors is as fruitless as ignoring them. Great interpretation is an offspring of courage, as well as of an awareness of what the music of the past has meant to the musicians of the relatively recent past. Farther than the memory of living men tradition cannot go, because even the written record (take Beethoven's own metronome marks, for instance, or Mozart's precepts of how to play the piano) makes no sense when the effect described has been forgotten.

Second-class French conductors, especially opera conductors, have often a thorough knowledge of how everything ought to go but lack the temperament for infusing their readings with animation. The more powerful conducting personalities in the France of today, Paray and Munch, for instance, often achieve animation by throwing overboard respect for even the composer's expressed intention, for all the world like any second-class Italian opera leader. Our own specialists of animation and beautiful sound are only a little more thoughtful. And they have at least the excuse of having passed their youth out of contact with a major musical tradition, of not having known the classics early enough to feel at home with them. The same is true of them with regard to the modern classics. Monteux and Ansermet remember the sense in Debussy and in the early Stravinsky ballets, the sense as well as the sound, because they were themselves, as young men, part of the modern movement. Most of the others either have forgotten what it was all about or never knew.

Leonard Bernstein knows what American music is all about, but the western European repertory he is obliged to improvise. When he follows a master with regard to it, he follows, moreover, a Russian, Koussevitzky, for whom it has always been foreign matter.

That is why, I think, he goes into such chorybantic ecstasies in front of it. He needs to mime, for himself and for others, a conviction that he does not have. He does no such act before American works of his own time. He takes them naturally, reads them with authority. Whether Bernstein will become in time a traditional conductor or a highly personal one is not easy to prophesy. He is a consecrated character, and his culture is considerable. It just might come about, though, that, having to learn classic repertory the hard way, which is after fifteen, and in a hurry, he would throw his cultural beginnings away and build toward success on a sheer talent for animation and personal projection. I must say he worries us all a little bit.

It would be disappointing if our brightest young leader should turn out to be just a star conductor in an age when bluff, temperament, and show-off are no longer effective on the concert stage. They have become, indeed, the privilege of management. Success, today and tomorrow, even financial success, depends on any artist's keeping his ego down to reasonable size. One of the best ways of accomplishing this is to keep one's mind on both the sound and the sense of the music one is playing. All the available knowledge there is about these matters constitutes the tradition. Neglecting to buttress his rising eminence with the full support of tradition is about the biggest mistake an American conductor in this generation could make.

October 19, 1947

Atonality Today (I)

Music that avoids classic scales and interval relations is now the chief region of organized advance. Ten years ago it might have been thought that this music was moribund, that its major achievements lay in the past, that its surviving practitioners and their progeny were a minor sectarian group, rigid, stalemated, immobilized by the complexity of their own syntax. Today it is clear that immobility is a danger facing rather the other schools of modernism than that which derives from Schönberg and that the young, far from being imprisoned by the twelve-tone syntax, are finding a new freedom through its discipline. More than that, they are engaged in research and experiment. Twelve-tone writing is not at all nowadays, if it ever was, a closed technique or a closed aesthetic. On the contrary, it is the main field of musical composition where progress is taking place.

This progress is now operating on an intercontinental, though not a world-wide, scale. Its adepts are numerous in the United States, in France, in Italy, in England, in Switzerland, in Argentina, and in Chile, but not, curiously enough, in Austria, the country of its origin, or in Germany, where its early expansion took place. These countries appear to be relatively quiescent just now with regard to the movement; and Soviet Russia, lately followed by the Iron Curtain countries, is quite out of the picture, technical research there in composition being at present under political ban. Los Angeles, where Arnold Schönberg lives, the founding father of it all, is a sort of Mount Athos to which pilgrimages are made. New York, London, and Venice (also Los Angeles and various European regional capitals) offer their concert privileges to atonal music. Paris, however, is the world center of its creation, analysis, criticism, publication, and propaganda.

Its most authoritative analyst and most widely read propagandist is René Leibowitz. Its chief Parisian creators are mostly the pupils of Olivier Messiaen, himself no twelve-toner at all. Its most intelligent critic, in my judgment, is Pierre Boulez, also a composer of phenomenal gifts. The publication most open to its exposition in detail is the quarterly magazine *Polyphonie*. This review, though only in its fifth issue, has already devoted a whole number to the tonal aspects of dodecaphony and another to musical rhythm in general, with especial attention to the rhythmic opportunities of twelve-tone composition. It is in the rhythmic domain, as a matter of fact, that music's chief advances are being made today; and the primacy of Paris right now in atonal music is due largely, I am sure, to its already affirmed position as the world center of rhythmic research. It is French rhythmic awareness, applied to the writing of twelve-tone music, that has lately initiated a second period in the development of the atonal, or to speak more correctly, the asymmetrical style.

The first period of this development, led by Arnold Schönberg and two of his pupils, Alban Berg and Anton Webern, saw the perfecting of a technique for avoiding classic tonal relations, for keeping the harmonic, the interval content of a piece fluid and of a uniform viscosity. In that technique rhythm is a free, a purely expressive element. The interval relations are very strict, however, homogeneity and the avoiding of all key systems requiring the almost constant presence, or at least the frequent restatement, of all twelve chromatic tones. The device of arranging these twelve tones in a special order, particular to each piece and consistent throughout it, is not an added complication of twelve-tone writing but a simplification, a rule of thumb that speeds up composition. The uses of such a "row," as it is called, are not necessarily intended for listeners to be aware of any more than the devices of fugal imitation are. They show up under analysis, of course, but they are mainly a composer's way of achieving thematic coherence with a minimum of effort.

No such row was present in atonal composition before the early 1920's, and it was Schönberg's invention. After that practically all atonal composers employed it, though with varying degrees of rigor. Nowadays some twelve-tone writers, like Boulez, will occasionally dispense with a fixed row altogether, or else, like the American Milton Babbitt, conceal it so throughly that only a skilled analy can unmask it. All such music, however, retains the thematic co herence of the more straightforward row music. It is a sophisticate form of atonality, not a primitive one.

The other chief simplifying device of the Schönbergian atonalists is the canon. Since atonal music, to be atonal, of necessity lacks the architectural strength provided by harmony, some system needed to be found for holding it together, for assuring at least a textura continuity. The only classical device of this kind not dependent on tonality is the canon. Consequently Schönberg adopted it and specified it in his simplification rules as the necessary concomitant in composition of any twelve-tone row. Such a row can be repeated canonically in four different orders—forward, backward, upside-down, and upsidedown backward. However, in the Schönberg system, since rhythm is always free, canonic strictness applies merely to the order in which the tones of the row appear, not to their length values. They can also appear vertically in chords, the row proceeding up-ward, downward, or both ways, but not in any tonal order other than its predetermined one.

Twelve-tone writing, at its simplest, consists therefore of the chromatic scale arranged in any nonrepeating order one wishes, that order, or row, being exposed in a series of canons. Classical rhythm and metrics are not forbidden. Neither is the imitation of classical harmonic and contrapuntal textures, though the absence of graded interval relations gives to these observances a purely rhythmic character. Twelve-tone music tends, in consequence, to-ward a rhythmically independent polyphony of equal voices.

According to Mr. Boulez, writing in *Polyphonie,* the twelve-tone-row technique is now perfected. Any composer can master it and can write by means of it in virtually complete avoidance of classical tone-relations. A new thing has been brought to completion. Or rather, let us say, to the first stage of completion. The next stage belongs to rhythm and to the working out of a technique for avoid-ing classical metrics. This second stage is the preoccupation of young twelve-tone composers everywhere. Its advanced front, how-ever, is the Paris group, because the Paris composing tradition has a backlog of researches in asymmetrical rhythm extending from Stravinsky's early ballets through Messiaen's recent innovations imported from India. An account of these will be our theme next Sunday.

January 29, 1950

Atonality Today (II)

Every century, as Lou Harrison once pointed out, has its chromatic and its diatonic style. Atonality is our chromatic style. Indeed, now that we have it in so highly evolved a form as twelve-tone composition, it seems to be the ultimate condition toward which chromatic harmony has always aspired. That condition is one of extreme fluidity, and its attraction for the pioneer-minded is that of the open sea. Classical scales and harmonic relations, in this conception, constitute reefs and treacherous currents and are hence to be avoided. Arnold Schönberg's twelve-tone-row syntax is a device for avoiding them. It is not the only one in existence, but it is the easiest to handle. Its simplicity and general practicability have caused its adoption by such a large majority among atonal writers that it may now be considered, I think, as the official, the orthodox method of composing in tones without composing in tonalities. Other methods, however excellent or even superior, constitute deviations from standard practice.

That practice is common to most of the mature music of atonality's Big Three—Schönberg, Berg, and Webern. Now two of these three are dead, and the other is seventy-five years old. Their favorite syntactical device, moveover, now available to all, is widely employed. Hence there is every reason to consider the epoch of advance that they represent to be a closed one. Certainly those of their musical progeny who work by identical or nearly identical methods bear the mark of the epigonous. Others, however, who accept the twelve-tone row and its canonic application as their basic method are not satisfied with this as a complete method. For them it is satisfactory only as a way of arranging tones with regard to their pitch. They wish a method equally convenient for ordering their length. Present-day efforts by twelve-tone composers to build a rhythmic technique comparable to their tonal system have initiated a second period in atonal research and composition.

If the first problem in atonality is to avoid familiar tonal relations, its second is surely to avoid familiar metrical ones. Complete renewal of the musical language and not a mere abandonment of its decayed portions, still less a spicing up of spoiled material, let us remember, is the aim of the atonal group. Also we must not forget that the Big Three, with slight exceptions in the work of Webern, made virtually no effort at originality in the rhythmic direction. Here they remained conservative, though less by principle, I should think, than from the fact that all advance needs to proceed in an orderly fashion, one thing at a time. The rhythmic achievements that now form the backlog of the second-period atonalists, the knowledge they start from, came almost wholly from outside the atonal tradition.

These are many. The exactly written-out rubato of Mahler, the fragmentated developments of Debussy, studies of Chinese, Javanese, East Indian, and other exotic musical systems, acquaintance with American ragtime and jazz, the epoch-marking Danse Sacrale from Stravinsky's *Rite of Spring* with its long, rhythmic phrases developed from tiny cells or rhythmic motifs, the experiments of Varése and others in pure percussion, the introduction into Western music by Messiaen of a Hindu device for varying a meter's minimum note-length—all have prepared the way for the new atonalists. Since the new rhythmic efforts have not yet brought about any standardization of rhythmic procedures, the field of rhythm is still full of sectarian dispute. Anybody with a new trick can imagine himself as in possession of the golden key. So far, however, there is no golden key. The period is a lively one, and all doors are still open, even to tonal writers.

The ideal of nonmetrical rhythm, like that of atonality, is asymmetry. Pierre Boulez states it as *d'éviter la carrure*, that is to say, the avoidance of everything square. This means that metrical repeating patterns are out and that even the rhythmic canon by inversion, the hardest to hear of all rhythmic imitations, requires violation of its exactitude by means of the Hindu added-dot. There are problems of rhythmic construction, too, that require solution, though conservative twelve-tone composers like René Leibowitz consider them subsidiary to tonal relations and not soluble independently. John Cage employs a numerical ratio in any piece between the phrase, the period, and the whole, the phrase occupying a time-measure which is the square root of the whole time and the periods occupying times proportional to those of the different rhythmic motifs within the phrase. This procedure, though it allows for asymmetry within the phrase and period, produces a tight symmetry in the whole composition and is not therefore quite the rendering of spontaneous emotion that the European atonalists hope to achieve.

The expressive aim of the atonalists has always been a romantic one, the depiction and provocation of intense, introverted feelings. Berg's music, in this respect, is closely related to that of Hugo Wolf and Mahler. Schönberg oscillates in his feeling allegiance between Wagner and Brahms. Both go into a waltz at the slightest pretext or even with none. Webern is more personal, more fastidious in his expression, as he is more original, more reflective in his applications of the twelve-tone technique. In both respects, and also through his pulverization of sound into a kind of luminous dust, he is an Austrian cousin of Debussy. He it is, in fact, and not Schönberg or Berg, whom the French atonalists tend most to revere and to stem from. He it is, too, who will probably remain most loved among the founding fathers when the atonal world shall have got round to doing over the art of instrumentation. But that will not be for another decade, at least. Just now a new rule of rhythm is the instrument lacking for traveling the trackless ocean of atonality, where the brave adventurer has, by the very nature of his renunciation, no harmony to guide him. The twelve-tone-row technique is a radar for avoiding shoreline hazards, but it has not yet taken any composer beyond the sight of Europe's historic monuments. For that a motor source will have to be found.

February 5, 1950

On Being American

What is an American composer? The Music Critics' Circle of New York City says it is any musical author of American citizenship. This group, however, and also the Pulitzer Prize Committee, as well as many other award-giving bodies, finds itself troubled in conscience about people like Stravinsky, Schönberg, and Hindemith. Can these composers be called American, whose styles were formed in Europe and whose most recent work, if it shows any influence of American ways and feeling, shows this certainly in no direction that could possibly be called nationalistic? Any award committee would think a second time before handing these men a certificate, as Americans, for musical excellence. The American section of the International Society for Contemporary Music has more than once been reproached in Europe for allowing the United States to be represented at international festivals of the society by composers of wholly European style and formation, such as Ernest Bloch and Ernst Krenek. And yet a transfer of citizenship cannot with justice be held to exclude any artist from the intellectual privileges of the country that has, both parties consenting, adopted him, no matter what kind of music he writes.

Neither can obvious localisms of style be demanded of any composer, native born or naturalized. If Schönberg, who writes in an ultra-chromatic and even atonal syntax and who practically never uses folk material, even that of his native Austria, is to be excluded by that fact from the ranks of American composers, then we must exclude along with him that stalwart Vermonter, Carl Ruggles, who speaks a not dissimilar musical language. And among the native-born young, Harold Shapero and Arthur Berger are no more American for writing in the international neoclassic manner (fountainhead Stravinsky) than Lou Harrison and Merton Brown are, who employ the international chromatic techniques (fountainhead Schönberg). All these gifted young writers of music are American composers, though none employs a nationalistic trademark or finds his best inspiration in our local folklore.

The fact is, of course, that citizens of the United States write music in every known style. There is no such thing, consequently, as an American style. There is not even a dominant style in American art music, as there is in our popular music. From the post-Romantic eclecticism of Howard Hanson and the post-Romantic expressionism of Bernard Rogers through the neoclassicized (if I may invent the word) impressionism of Edward Burlingame Hill and John Alden Carpenter, the strictly Parisian neoclassicism of Walter Piston, the romanticized neoclassicism of Roy Harris and William Schuman, the elegant neo-Romanticism of Samuel Barber, the sentimental neo-Romanticism of David Diamond, the folksy neo-Romanticism of Douglas Moore, Randall Thompson, and Henry Cowell, the Germano-eclectic modernism of Roger Sessions, the neo-primitive polytonalism of Charles Ives, and the ecstatic chromaticism of Carl Ruggles, to the percussive and rhythmic research fellows Edgar Varèse and John Cage, we have everything. We have also the world famous European atonalists Schönberg and Krenek, the neoclassic masters Stravinsky and Hindemith. We have, moreover, a national glory in the form of Aaron Copland, who so skillfully combines, in the Bartók manner, folk feeling with neoclassic techniques that foreigners often fail to recognize his music as American at all.

All this music is American, nevertheless, because it is made by Americans. If it has characteristic traits that can be identified as belonging to this continent only, our composers are largely unconscious of them. These are shared, moreover, by composers of all the schools and probably by our South American neighbors. Two devices typical of American practice (I have written about these before) are the nonaccelerating crescendo and a steady ground-rhythm of equalized eighth notes (expressed or not). Neither of these devices is known to Europeans, though practically all Americans take them for granted. Further study of American music may reveal other characteristics. But there can never be any justice in demanding their presence as a proof of musical Americanism. Any American has the right to write music in any way he wishes or is able to do. If the American school is beginning to be visible to Europeans as something not entirely provincial with regard to Vienna and Paris, something new, fresh, real, and a little strange, none of this novel quality is a monopoly, or even a specialty, of any group among us. It is not limited to the native-born or to the German-trained or to the French-influenced or to the self-taught or to the New-York-resident or to the California-bred. It is in the air and belongs to us all. It is a set of basic assumptions so common that everybody takes them for granted. This is why, though there is no dominant style in American music, there is, viewed from afar (say from Europe), an American school.

National feelings and local patriotisms are as sound sources of inspiration as any other. They are not, however, any nobler than any other. At best they are merely the stated or obvious subject of a piece. Music that has life in it always goes deeper than its stated subject or than what its author thought about while writing it. Nobody becomes an American composer by thinking about America while composing. If that were true Georges Auric's charming fox trot *Adieu New-York* would be American music and not French music, and *The Road to Mandalay* would be Burmese. The way to write American music is simple. All you have to do is to be an American and then write any kind of music you wish. There is precedent and model here for all the kinds. And any Americanism worth bothering about is everybody's property anyway. Leave it in the unconscious; let nature speak.

Nevertheless, the award-giving committees do have a problem on their hands. I suggest they just hedge and compromise for a while. That, after all, is a way of being American, too.

January 25, 1948

Too Many Languages

The kind of program that vocalists, particularly the younger ones, feel obliged to offer in their recitals is a formula that has long seemed to this reviewer ill suited to advancing either musical or technical excellence. Its fault can be stated in three words—*too many languages*. Not long ago, speaking before a meeting of voice teachers, he reproached them with responsibility for its continued observance and asked why so stupid a violation of all sense, pedagogical and artistic, had ever become established in custom. They answered in unanimity, "We do not know, and we do not approve it." Nevertheless, every aspiring singer in our midst feels obliged to offer in recital an Italian, a German, a French, and an English group of songs.

Naturally, they sing all these languages badly, even, in many cases, English. Often, having merely learned their foreign songs phonetically, they have only an approximate idea of the texts' meaning. The communication of poetry under such circumstances is quite impossible. It is not easy, either, to sing agreeably when the full content of the composer's feelings, as embodied in verbal values, is not clear to the interpreter. Moreover, nobody demands this monkey-like behavior. The public does not like it; the press does not like it; and managements care only for what the audience and the press like. Singing teachers, who are responsible for the tradition and its preservation, all know it is opposed to good artistic standards. And yet they hesitate to do away with it. Several of them have suggested that since music schools in America require of singers three languages besides English, if a degree is to be awarded, they themselves are the victims of a circumstance. But it is the singing teachers who determine, finally, degree requirements for singers. Surely they could demand revision of a faulty curriculum.

Such a curriculum is faulty because it is not a preparation for professional life. Few professional vocalists of the first class ever sing four languages in public. The best usually sing two, their own and one other. Knowing one foreign language gives depth and discrimination to an artist's handling of his own. Helen Traubel, by specializing in German repertory, has had a great career. Mary Garden did the same with French, Jan Peerce and Richard Tucker with Italian. A language means something in the mouths of these artists. They know its feel, its style, its nature, its relation to life and to

190

music. A few singers have the gift of tongues; but for every Jennie Tourel in the world, there are a dozen Lotte Lehmanns, Pinzas, and Carusos, for whom a new language has to be approached slowly, circumspectly, once in a lifetime.

A young singer needs to know, for studio purposes, the Italian vowels, because they are pure. He needs also to sing (and translation will do) enough French, German, and Italian songs to acquire an acquaintance with these musical literatures. Then he should choose one for his own. He should adopt a country, speak its language, read its books, live among its people, eat its food. In this way he may learn to interpret its music with understanding. As he advances in professional life, travels, and reads, he may find it useful to pick up a smattering of other languages, including Spanish and Russian. But he does not have to sing them, and he should not sing them until he feels thoroughly at home with their sound and with their sense. An occasional compliment to local audiences will be enough exception to prove the value of this rule.

All this time he should be singing his own language, learning it, loving it, making its sounds behave, and making the farthest ticket-holder hear what he says. This is the way singers work abroad, and it is the right way. Any other is injurious and silly. Requiring young vocalists to sing four languages is like asking string players to be equally proficient on the violin, the viola, and the cello. Such acrobatics should be discouraged.

If any person reading this column knows any reason why the four-language formula should be further tolerated by teachers or by concert-goers, I hope he will correct my impatience. In my view, and the voice teachers met in convention did seem to agree with me, it is unmusical, unintelligent, inartistic, and pedagogically unsound.

April 23, 1950

High Costs

The depression has hit the music business and no doubt about it. Records, books, and concert tickets are getting harder and harder to sell; and the money for giving prestige recitals in New York is far less plentiful than it was during the war and just after. The cost of such recitals, moreover, has about doubled in the last three years. A Town Hall event, professionally managed and publicized modestly, used to cost the artist about a thousand dollars. It now comes to nearer two thousand. Costs are higher all round; but no management, aware of the public's diminished purchasing power, dares ask us to pay higher prices for admission. Buyer resistance is already formidable. Only a few nationally-advertised artists and organizations can today fill any New York hall without resorting to "paper."

Even rich organizations like the Philadelphia Orchestra and the Metropolitan Opera Association have threatened suicide. I must say they have brought their troubles on themselves. Not that any group in the country is solely responsible for the rise in prices, not even Congress. But it has long been evident that artistic enterprises which conduct their operations on the models of business must accept the unhappy consequences of a business depression. If our symphony orchestras were more clearly a part of our real cultural life, like the universities, and less a mere front for the music industries, for radio, recording, and concert management, they would be in a better position than they are today to face deficits. Their intellectual function would be worth more as capital. As I remarked several years ago about the Metropolitan Opera, such groups do best when they conduct themselves and think of themselves as successful money-spending enterprises, not as unsuccessful money-making ones.

Neither should they get mixed up in class warfare. It is unfortunate that supposedly philanthropic and cultural foundations serving art and public instruction should appear in the role of labor's enemy. They should economize where and when they can, naturally; and they should negotiate the most favorable contracts they can. They should not waste their funds. But neither should they assume before the whole public any attitude that renders the motivation of their trustees and administrators suspect to a large part of that public, namely, to all those citizens, many of them music consumers, who make up the trade union movement or who believe in its value to our economy.

I mean by this that the negotiation of labor contracts between unions and nonprofit-making institutions should be carried on without recourse to the major arms of the labor-capital struggle. Symphony orchestras have gone on strike in the past, but rarely successfully; and the action has usually, as in the case of the Boston Symphony Orchestra's strike back in 1920, been costly to unionism in terms of public opinion. The Metropolitan Opera's threat of last August to suspend operations and the Philadelphia Orchestra's announcement of last Monday, canceling its whole concert season, risk a similar unfavorable result for management, since both are dangerously close to what is called in industry a lockout. (In neither case was complete liquidation of the enterprise proposed.) That Philadelphia's Local 77 of the Musicians' Union so understood the move was clear from their reply that they were "unwilling and unable" to accept the orchestra board's decision. Both sides left the door open to further negotiation.

The present writer is holding no brief for either contestant. He is simply pointing out that two philanthropic musical enterprises have recently risked unfavorable public opinion by behaving as if they were businesses, as if no obligation to the public had ever been assumed, as if their governing boards were free to discontinue a valued cultural operation on no other provocation than that of a threatened deficit. It is such a board's duty to negotiate contracts, accept the results, and meet deficits. It is also their privilege to call for public support in meeting deficits. It is their duty, moreover, to ask for such support, to give the public its chance to pay up, before cavalierly announcing the interruption of a public service.

The Philadelphia management has long complained that the Musicians' Union local takes to itself an unfair negotiating advantage by delaying each year to propose its terms until just before the season opens. The union, too, may well at present consider the orchestra's directors to have acted unfairly in threatening the public with a stoppage of the concerts merely to avoid the trouble of raising the money for a wage increase. Wage increases are everywhere in discussion; in a time of high prices their demand need surprise no one. Whether granted or not, they have to be considered. I know nothing of the horse trading that must certainly have gone on between management and the union in Philadelphia, or what exasperation provoked the orchestra board to cancel, at least in announcement, its whole concert season. I merely repeat that I find the gesture unbecoming, as was certainly that of the Metropolitan Opera board in threatening last summer to omit a season from its history.

I find the gesture unbecoming because it uses us, the public, as a pawn in the game of costs. We do not care what symphony orchestras cost; our interest is in what and how they play. If an administration is efficient (and one has every reason to believe that Philadelphia's is), then the proper price of musicians, like that of railway fares, hall rent, musical scores, trucking, and publicity, is simply whatever such a management can get the best for, no more and no less. If prices all round are more than we, the public, are able to cope with, then we do without an orchestra or put up with a cheaper one. But we do not like having trustees tell us they are stopping our concerts simply because they find some necessary element of the enterprise, in their opinion, overpriced. What have they in mind as their trust, one wonders, when they assume what is, after all, our privilege? Are they acting as trustees of all our interests and of music's place in the intellectual tradition, or are they merely playing trustees of private capital in capital's age-old war with labor?

October 3, 1948

194

The Oratorio Style

Spring always brings forth choral festivities. Many of these involve soloists. Most of the latter are less effective than one would wish. The circumstances that war against musical efficiency on the part of soloists are many. Chief among them is the fact that standing on the same level with an accompanying orchestra puts vocalists at a disadvantage. Even so skillfull a conductor as Toscanini cannot prevent a platform orchestra from occasionally overpowering the voice. If the choral "big machines" could be given in an opera house, with the orchestra in a pit, the solos would be easier to project.

Another trouble is the inability of middle-sized orchestras to play softly (there rarely being room either on the platform or in the budget for a full contingent of strings). A very small group, chamber-music size, can play pianissimo; and so can a full symphony orchestra with thirty-two or more violins. But a middle-sized orchestra cannot do it. Acoustical facts are involved, and so is a certain auditory illusion; the matter merits study before a true explanation of the phenomenon can be advanced. But conductors are acquainted with it. Stated roughly it amounts to this, that a large orchestra can play softer than a small one. Oratorio orchestras are rarely big enough to play a real pianissimo. And soloists, especially when standing right beside an orchestra, have need often of a really pianissimo accompaniment.

A third offender is the "oratorio style" itself. This is a faulty conception of how soloists should interpret a sacred text to orchestral accompaniment in a large hall. There is no one style suitable to all such works. The idea that something halfway between a broad operatic manner and an intimate recital refinement will do merely makes for a style that is neither one thing nor the other. What you get mostly is a manner of execution lacking the vocal refinements of recital art and the expressivity of the theater. The only valid part of the so-called "oratorio style" is the maxim that personal expressivity, impersonation, is inappropriate to texts, sacred or secular, that involve no impersonation.

Now there is such a thing, and very beautiful it is, as the Handelian style. It works for Handel's operas as well as for his oratorios. It also works, with tenderness added, for the Mendelssohn oratorios, which are designed after those of Handel. It does not work for Bach or Haydn or Mozart or Beethoven or Brahms and still less for Rossini, Berlioz, Verdi, Honegger, or Stravinsky. A good rule of thumb is to approach any composer's concert works of large format (works for chorus, vocal soloists, and orchestra) in the same manner as one would approach his stage works. When, as in the case of Bach and Brahms, there are no stage works to give the cue, other criteria must be found. But roughly speaking, any composer's stage style is the touchstone to his works for similar musical forces.

Thus it comes about that Beethoven's Missa Solemnis gives a better effect when read as a version of his *Fidelio*, impersonation omitted, than when read as an emulation of Handel's *Messiah* or of Mendelssohn's *Elijah*. Haydn's *Creation* and *The Seasons* should be evocative and pastoral, like most of his operas. Berlioz's Requiem is not very different from *The Trojans* or from his *Romeo and Juliet* or *The Damnation of Faust*. Verdi's Requiem is certainly not far from *La Forza del Destino* or Mozart's Requiem from *The Magic Flute*. Debussy's *Prodigal Son* and *Blessed Damozel* (the latter not a sacred text at all) are of the family of *Pelléas*, not of *Judas Maccabeus*. Stravinsky's *Oedipus Rex* is by the author of *Les Noces* and *L'Histoire d'un Soldat;* and though the Handelian style is certainly here evoked, it is evoked only, not at any point directly employed.

Brahms has given us no stage clew to his choral works, but he has left a huge body of songs greatly resembling them. My recommendation to conductors is to read the *German Requiem* as sensitively and as intimately as if it were *Mainacht* or the *Sapphische Ode*. And the Bach Passions, Christmas Oratorio, and Mass in B-minor were unquestionably composed, like the same author's church cantatas, for small choral bodies and with chamber-style instrumentation. Their dominating quality is less the massiveness of certain choral effects than their extreme floridity everywhere or, in the case of the Passions, their tenderness and intimacy.

A grander and more elegant Handelian style than is currently available would be welcome in our concert halls. It would not be difficult to achieve, either, if our singers and conductors would try a little harder, because its characteristics are nowhere in dispute. I should even like to see the Handelian style used as the bedrock of vocal training, since Handel offers the best-written body of vocal music available to English-speaking singers. But this does not mean that the Handelian style should be applied willy-nilly to the whole chorus-with-soloists repertory. Its indiscriminate application in England is, indeed, the origin of that false concept "the oratorio style." The continentals make no such error. That is why Walter and Monteux and occasionally Koussevitzky give us regularly such delightful readings of the choral classics, while our own conductors, influenced by the false concept of an "oratorio style" that excuses every fault but lack of loudness, give us year after year performances of the chorus-with-soloists repertory that are styleless, inaccurate, and inexpressive. The soloists are somewhat at fault, too, though not entirely. They can do better work than they generally do; what they chiefly need is conductors who know what they want to hear and how to ask for it. You cannot, of course, produce an oratorio properly, any more than you can an opera, by rehearsing only the choral passages.

May 9, 1948

The Catholic Church Accepts Modern Music

Pope Pius X's encyclical of November 22, 1903, entitled *Motu Proprio,* which dealt with church music and the proper manner of its performance, was a revolutionary document. Its radical pronouncements were three: (1) Gregorian chant was declared the official and true music of the Roman Catholic liturgy; (2) the sixteenth-century "Roman school" of polyphony (or Palestrina style), ordained as appropriate for the grander ceremonies of the church in connection with certain texts of the liturgy, was so nominated for its derivation from Gregorian chant and its adherence to the spirit of this; and (3) musical styles associated with the opera, which means, in practice, all musical styles developed after 1600, were condemned as non-liturgical, irrespective of their intrinsic musical merits. Masses composed by such sound Catholics as Mozart, Rossini, Schubert, Bruckner, and César Franck were thus removed from Church usage, along with sacred settings of the Sextet from *Lucia di Lammermoor*, the Drinking Song from *Lucrezia Borgia*, and Liszt's *Liebestraum, No. 1*, all of which, believe it or not, were in those days both current and popular.

From that time to our own, Catholic church music has been marked by a sobriety, a seemliness, and a decorum that have gradually come to give the tone, the acceptable tone, to all the church music of Western Christendom, wherever this follows reflected procedures rather than folk patterns. Nevertheless, that whole revision of musical syntax that has been our century's most impressive contribution to the art has begun to creep into Catholic services and to add to the mystic medievalism of Gregorian chant and to the Counter-Reformation-style humanism of Palestrinian polyphony a definitely contemporary, a twentieth-century note. This came earliest in France, through the Parisian organists, whose improvisations, from Vierne to Messiaen, have long followed, with archiepiscopal toleration, the most advanced procedures of composition.

Contemporary church architecture and decoration, moreover, have tended everywhere, save perhaps in the United States, toward liberation from the antimodernist papal influence of the last fifty years, which, if it gave to the plastic side of devotion, as to liturgical music, an incomparable criterion of taste, limited the living creators of ecclesiastical art to imitating the antique. Certain bishops have been more lenient than others, however, in the application of the law;

and little by little churches of reinforced concrete, on the cheap scale, and churches designed and decorated by celebrated modern artists, on the expensive scale, have been rearing their modernistic heads over the landscape. The French Dominicans, who have been for some time the spearhead of a movement within the Church toward proselytizing twentieth-century intellectuals through friendliness toward twentieth-century intellectual manifestations, have probably been no less influential of late on papal thought than has the exigency of rebuilding ruined ecclesiastical edifices all over Europe at the lowest possible cost.

In any case, Pope Pius XII has come out for modernism in the arts. The encyclical of November 20, 1947, entitled *Mediator Dei,* in which his acceptance of modernism is incorporated, is no such revolutionary document as the *Motu Proprio* of 1903, which condemned, for church usage, most of the music written since 1585. Its subject is the liturgy as a whole; and it reasserts, as regards music, two of the basic precepts of the earlier pronouncement. The Gregorian chant is to remain the "true music" of the service, and congregational participation in this is to be encouraged. On the other hand, where the *Motu Proprio* allowed the congregational use of regional-style hymns only on condition that these seem not irreverent to persons from other regions, the *Mediator Dei* recommends them with no such reserve. And the Palestrina (or "Roman") style is not mentioned.

The blessing of modern music reads as follows (I translate from the Italian version of the Pope's Latin text, as published in *L'Oservatore Romano,* Vatican City, December 1, 1947, since no official complete English version of the encyclical has yet arrived in this country) : "It cannot be asserted . . . that modern music, instrumental and vocal (*la musica e il canto moderno*), should be excluded altogether from Catholic worship. Therefore, unless this is profane in character or unseemly of expression with respect to holy places and sacred service, or derived from a vain research for unusual and outlandish effects, it is necessary surely to open to it the doors of our churches, since both kinds of it [instrumental and vocal] can contribute in no small way to the splendor of the holy rites, to the elevation of the mind, and . . . to true devotion." A similar blessing follows of modern architecture, painting, sculpture, and decoration, with regard to their use in churches.

There is little more to be said. Modern music is now official to the Roman Church, the very fount and center of musical conservatism. Long ago it was received in the schools, by the theater, at the subscription concerts. No major musical power is today vowed to musical reaction save the Soviet government and possibly the American films. Either might do a U-turn tomorrow. And the contemporary musical world has long since learned to get on without both. Not, however, without the Church. Her reserve we have always regretted. There are still minor points to be decided, of course. How far, for instance, can twelve-tone-row music be called "a vain research"? And may not, perhaps, repetitions of the text and instruments of percussion, if tastefully introduced, be returned discreetly to liturgical custom? All such matters will be decided in the Church by papal counsel and by conferences, in other institutions by custom. But the schism is healed. Not in our lifetime will modern music ever again be seriously a problem to anyone living between the Iron Curtain and Los Angeles.

For church practice, I gather that the Pope wishes the Gregorian chant, its study and practice, to remain the Church's musical main foundation, and that the monotony and somewhat recondite character of this be relieved on the simpler religious occasions by hymn singing, on the grander ones by set-pieces of contemporary composition. Palestrina and his school are not to be ejected, nor is the florid music of Mozart and other composers whose manner has theatrical or profane associations yet to be taken back. What any music director can get by with, as modernism, will continue to depend on the culture of his local pastor and the enlightenment of his bishop. But an order from Rome is an order. Little by little you will be hearing, along with the plainsong, a new kind of music in Catholic churches. And the world-wideness with which the Catholic Church operates in liturgical matters cannot fail to lend to its new repertory an influence on Protestant music. It is probable, indeed, that in opening the doors of his Church to musical advance the Pope

200

has spoken, how consciously I could not say, for the whole Judeo-Christian world, at least for the intellectual confraternity within it that holds the children of the twentieth century entitled to speak their own language without shame. To speak it, moreover, not only among themselves but also to God.

February 1, 1948

INDEX

Abravanel, Maurice, 77
Academy of Music (Philadelphia), 70
Accordion Teachers Guild, 142-3
Adam, Adolphe, 94
Aitken, Webster, 35-6
Akhmatova, Anna, 155-6
Albéniz, Isaac, 30
  Albaicín, El, 30
  Triana, 30
Alvary, Lorenzo, 142
Anderson, Marian, 171
Anderson, Maxwell, 131
Ansermet, Ernest, 9-10, 92, 93, 170, 179
Antheil, George, 109
  Symphony No. 5, 109
Aquinas, St. Thomas, 162
Arnold, Thurman, 75
Asafiev, Boris, 165

Aubert, Louis, 101
  Offrande, 101-2
Auric, Georges, 120, 189
  Adieu New York, 189

B.B.C. Third Program, 148
Babbitt, Milton, 182
Bach, Johann Sebastian, 5, 23, 33, 34, 39, 40, 41, 43, 46, 90, 118, 125, 137, 196-7
  Christmas Oratorio, 196-7
  Concerto for Violin and Orchestra, G minor, 90
  Mass, B minor, 196-7
  Partita, D minor, for Violin alone, 39-40
  Passions, 196-7
  Prelude and Fugue, A minor, for Organ (transcribed by Liszt), 33, 34
  Suite "Discordable," C minor, 45
    Prelude and Fugue, 45
  Suite, D, for Cello alone, 43
  Toccata and Fugue, D minor (transcribed by Ormandy), 5
Bakaleinikoff, Vladimir, 145
Ballet Russe (Diaghilev), 165
Balsam, Arthur, 40
Barber, Samuel, 188
Barraine, Elsa, 111
  Symphony No. 2, 111
Barraud, Henry, 20, 130
Bartók, Béla, 13, 110, 117, 127, 132-4, 175, 176, 188
  Concerto for Orchestra, 13, 134
  string quartets, 134, 176
Beecham, Sir Thomas, 23-6, 170
Beethoven, Ludwig van, 2, 7, 9, 13, 14, 33, 36, 37, 40, 85-6, 89, 94, 102, 108, 109, 146, 175, 179, 196
  concertos for piano and orchestra
    No. 4, 13, 14
    No. 5, 89
  Fidelio, 146, 196
    overture, 146
  Missa Solemnis, 196

206